School

SCHOOL OF THOUGHT

101 Great Liberal Thinkers

EAMONN BUTLER

Institute of
Economic Affairs

First published in Great Britain in 2019 by
The Institute of Economic Affairs
2 Lord North Street
Westminster
London SW1P 3LB
in association with London Publishing Partnership Ltd
www.londonpublishingpartnership.co.uk

The mission of the Institute of Economic Affairs is to improve understanding
of the fundamental institutions of a free society by analysing and expounding
the role of markets in solving economic and social problems.

A CIP catalogue record for this book is available from the British Library.

ISBN 978-0-255-36776-9

Many IEA publications are translated into languages other
than English or are reprinted. Permission to translate or to reprint
should be sought from the Director General at the address above.

Typeset in Kepler by T&T Productions Ltd
www.tandtproductions.com

Printed and bound in Great Britain by Page Bros

CONTENTS

THE THINKERS

Ancient liberal thinkers

Early modern thinkers

Revolutionaries and radicals

The age of reform

[59] William Lloyd Garrison (1805–1879)
Abolitionism; women's rights; passive resistance

[60] John Stuart Mill (1806–1873)
*Choice and responsibility; tyranny of the majority;
the no-harm principle*

[61] Harriet Taylor Mill (1807–1858)
Female education and suffrage; worker co-ownership

[62] Lysander Spooner (1808–1887)
*Deregulation and competition; vices are not crimes;
anarchism*

[63] Henry David Thoreau (1817–1862)
*Civil disobedience; anarchism; abolitionism;
injustice of majority voting*

[64] Frederick Douglass (1818–1895)
Abolitionism; human choice and responsibility

[65] Gustave de Molinari (1819–1912)
*Anarcho-capitalism; critique of state, power and
privilege; private security*

[66] Herbert Spencer (1820–1903)
*Freedom and progress; evolution of society;
political rights; universal suffrage*

[67] John Elliott Cairnes (1823–1875)
*Economic method; imperfect competition; economic
deficiencies of slavery*

[68] Edward Atkinson (1827–1905)
Abolitionism; anti-imperialism; free trade

[69] Josephine Butler (1828–1906)
*Liberal feminism; emancipation; reform of
prostitution laws*

The modern era

The free economy and society

ABOUT THE AUTHOR

Eamonn Butler is Director of the Adam Smith Institute, one of the world's leading policy think tanks. He holds degrees in economics and psychology, a PhD in philosophy, and an honorary DLitt. In the 1970s he worked in Washington for the US House of Representatives, and taught philosophy at Hillsdale College, Michigan, before returning to the UK to help found the Adam Smith Institute. A former winner of the Freedom Medal awarded by Freedoms Foundation of Valley Forge and the UK National Free Enterprise Award, Eamonn is currently Secretary of the Mont Pelerin Society.

Eamonn is the author of many books, including introductions to the pioneering economists and thinkers Adam Smith, Milton Friedman, F. A. Hayek, Ludwig von Mises and Ayn Rand. He has also published primers on classical liberalism, public choice, Magna Carta and the Austrian School of Economics, as well as *The Condensed Wealth of Nations* and *The Best Book on the Market*. His *Foundations of a Free Society* won the 2014 Fisher Prize. He is co-author of *Forty Centuries of Wage and Price Controls*, and of a series of books on IQ. He is a frequent contributor to print, broadcast and online media.

1 INTRODUCTION

What this book is about

This book profiles the lives and ideas of some of the leading thinkers on individual liberty, from ancient times up to today.

These *liberals* – to use the word in the European (not the American) sense – all see the top priorities of political, social and economic life as being to maximise individual freedom and minimise the use of force. But they vary in their precise views on how to achieve this and how large any government role should be. Some see little or no need for the state. Many argue that some government authority is required, particularly in the provision of defence, policing and justice. Others see an even wider role for government in social or economic life.

Who this book is for

This book is primarily for intelligent lay readers who are interested in the public debate on politics, government, social institutions, capitalism, rights, liberty and morality, and who want to understand the pro-freedom side of the debate. It is designed for those who broadly understand the principles of a free society, but want to know more about the ideas, thinkers and schools of thought that have shaped the concept. It aims to provide this knowledge in plain words with no academic-style footnotes, references or glossaries.

Nevertheless, it also gives school and university students of economics, politics, ethics and philosophy a concise introduction into a set of radical ideas and the thinkers responsible. There is plenty in here to stimulate informed and critical debate on how society is and should be structured.

How this book is laid out

After outlining the main elements of liberal thought, the book sketches liberal thinkers in order of their date of birth. This gives the reader some impression of how liberal ideas evolved over time. But the course of liberal thought is not a straight path. Liberalism is not a set doctrine, but a series of ongoing debates. Often there is progress on one issue, which is then parked for decades, until some other thinker puts a new twist on it. In addition, some thinkers have contributed ideas on many different subjects. So, there is no perfect way to list liberalism's thinkers. But since the aim of this book is to profile the individuals and their contributions, a chronological approach has been chosen.

2 LIBERALISM AND LIBERAL THINKERS

The thinkers in this book are *not* what most Americans call 'liberals'. While both groups share the priority of personal freedom, American liberals support far more state intervention in social and economic life in order to achieve it. Such interventions may include wealth or income redistribution, special support and protection for workers and industries, providing a wide range of public goods, regulating markets and seeking to protect people from their own actions.

Though the liberals listed here feel just as much for the welfare of others, they are wary of such policies. They see them as threats to freedom – giving too much power to authorities and treating citizens like dependent children rather than free adults – and believe that government interventions can (and usually do) have unforeseen, damaging consequences.

What is a liberal?

A number of key principles unify liberals in this sense.

Maximising freedom. Liberals believe that we should try to *maximise individual freedom*. People should be free to live as they want and where they want, choose their beliefs, be able to speak freely, trade with each other, assemble together, take part in politics, own property, keep what they produce, and live without the threat of arbitrary arrest or detention or harm. They should face only the *minimum necessary restraint* from other individuals or authorities.

Priority of the individual. Second, liberals see the *individual as more important than the collective*. Only individuals have ambitions, purposes and interests. Groups do not: they are merely collections of individuals. When we sacrifice the interests of individuals to what some authority or expert or political leader says is the interest of society, individuals are exposed to the threat of tyranny.

Toleration. Third, liberals advocate *toleration* – that we should not restrict people's actions just because we disapprove of them or disagree with them. Everyone should be free to hold their own opinions, speak their minds and live as they choose, even if others consider those opinions and words and lifestyle immoral or offensive. People should be free to assemble in clubs, unions or political parties, even if others think them subversive crackpots. They should be free to trade goods and services, including ones (such as drugs, gambling and prostitution) that are widely disapproved of. And they should be free to practise whatever religion they want, even if the vast majority disapprove.

Minimising coercion. Fourth, liberals wish to *minimise coercion*. They want a world where we get along by peaceful agreement, not one where people use force or the threat of force to subjugate others. They maintain that the judicial authority of the state, its power to tax or fine or imprison or otherwise coerce citizens, must be kept to its essential minimum: for as **Lord Acton** noted, power tends to corrupt.

Representative and limited government. Fifth, while some thinkers on the liberal spectrum see no use for government at all, most liberals believe there is an important role for the state. But it is a limited role – to defend individuals against violence and theft, either from other citizens or from abroad, and to dispense justice when theft or violence occurs.

When choosing those who decide what the exact rules should be and how to enforce them, most liberals advocate *representative and constitutional democracy.* This, they say, makes it clear that government derives its authority only from the individuals who create it. Government is their servant, not their master. A constitution that specifies how official power may *not* be used, and free elections in which representatives can be removed from office, are the best means yet found for maintaining this relationship.

Rule of law. Sixth, liberals insist on the *rule of law.* Laws should apply equally to everyone, regardless of gender, race, religion, language, family or any other irrelevant characteristics. And they should apply to government officers just as much as to ordinary people. To safeguard this principle, and prevent those in power manipulating the law for their own benefit, there must be basic judicial principles such as equal treatment, habeas corpus, trial by jury, due process and proportionate punishments.

Spontaneous order. Seventh, liberals argue that human institutions mostly arise spontaneously, rather than through conscious planning. Nobody deliberately invented markets, the price system, money, language, the rules of justice or the common law. They simply grew and evolved out of the countless interactions between individuals, because they were useful.

Like a footpath that is trodden down as waves of people seek the easiest route across a field, such institutions are the result of *human action, but not of human design.* They are examples of *spontaneous order* – structures that are often highly complex, but need no guiding authorities to create and manage them. Indeed, government action is more likely to disrupt them than rationalise them.

Free markets. Eighth, liberals hold that wealth is created by the mutual cooperation of individuals in the spontaneous order of the marketplace. Prosperity comes through individuals inventing, creating, saving, investing and exchanging things for mutual benefit. Our economic order grows out of simple rules, such as honesty and respect for property.

Civil society. Ninth, liberals believe that voluntary associations provide people's social needs better than governments. While they emphasise the priority of individuals, they recognise that individuals are also members of families and of groups such as clubs, associations, unions, religions, schools, online communities, campaigns and charities. These spontaneous institutions of *civil society* give us greater and far richer opportunities for collaboration than the clumsy institutions deliberately created by centralised governments.

Doubts about power. Lastly, liberals are concerned about the corrupting effects of political power. They see the most difficult problem for a free society not as how to dispense power, but how to restrain those who are given it. They know that politicians and officials are not angels, nor impartial defenders of the public interest. Rather, all have their own interests – and the temptation to use political power to advance those private interests is strong.

What is a liberal thinker?

In summary, liberals believe in a thriving, spontaneous social order with mutual respect, toleration, non-aggression, cooperation and voluntary exchange between free people. Most base this on individuals' basic moral rights of life, liberty and property, protected by a strong, trustworthy justice system. They favour free speech, free association, the rule of law and limits on government that prevent people in authority violating individual freedoms. But liberalism remains a broad spectrum of views, and liberals do disagree on many issues.

Some of the key classical liberal debates

The key question for liberals is what, if anything, justifies curbing a person's freedom. Clearly, people cannot be permitted to do *anything* they please, as that would violate the similar freedom of others: your liberty to swing your fist, for example, extends no further than my nose. Nor, for the same reason, can people be free to harm others through robbery, fraud or physical assault. But many liberals accept that the greater good might require some *additional* curbs on freedom – forcing people to pay taxes for defence, justice and public works for example, or preventing them from polluting other people's air and water.

Freedom and the public good. That leaves the questions of what exactly the greater, 'public' good is, who decides it, and what restraints are justified in order to achieve it. Liberals have different answers: some argue that 'social utility' calls for a number of restrictions on liberty; others argue that nothing justifies any such curbs. Yet liberals agree that the presumption should be in favour of liberty, and that those seeking to restrict freedom must come up with convincing reasons. They also agree that it is unwise to let governments decide these issues – because governments will tend to advocate more government and less freedom.

The nature and limits of rights. Some liberals suggest that *individual rights* set the limits on how far our freedom can be curtailed. They insist that the rights to life, liberty, conscience and property cannot be violated by anyone, including governments. But this raises the same questions of what exactly these rights are and who decides the matter – and where rights come from, what responsibilities they impose on others, when they can be overridden, and what justifies them.

Some liberals see rights as part of what human beings are; some think them justified by their social usefulness or the general happiness; some see them as moral principles that protect us from the ravages of unlimited government (albeit principles that are open to debate); others question whether rights exist at all. But those who do accept the idea of individual rights agree that they can be overridden only in exceptional circumstances, and that any violation of those rights must always be well justified.

Curbing power. Most liberals believe that there is *some* role for the use of force by the state. That opens up further debates, on the purpose and limit of this authority and how to keep it within bounds. To that end, liberals favour a rule of law that prevents the arbitrary use of state power. Some stress that a state's authority comes only from the individuals whom it serves – and that those individuals may legitimately revolt if government exceeds this authority. But again: when exactly is that?

There are no settled answers to any of these and many other questions. One certainty, however, is that liberals have been, and remain, energetic and innovative in debating them.

3 ANCIENT LIBERAL THINKERS

Early origins of liberalism

Freedom is a universal idea. It has strong roots in almost all religions and cultures, from Taoism through Islam to Buddhism; and across the world, from Asia through the Middle East to the West.

The ancient Chinese scholar **[1] Laozi**, sometimes rendered Lao-Tzu or Lao-Tze (*c.*600 BC), was the founder of Taoism. In his work *Tao Te Ching*, he argued that human life was the result of a complex balance of different forces. A ruler who interfered with this balance risked unintended consequences. 'Meddling and touching everything will work badly and prove disappointing', he wrote:

> Without law or compulsion, men would dwell in harmony ... The more prohibitions there are, the poorer the people will be. The more laws that are promulgated, the more thieves and bandits there will be. Therefore a sage ruler says: 'I will do nothing purposefully, and the people will transform themselves. I will prefer to keep still, and the people will themselves become correct. I will take no trouble, and the people will become rich by themselves ...'

In Europe, classical Greece and ancient Rome were not liberal societies. Even in 'democratic' Athens, only a small minority actually made the decisions. People were expected to subjugate their individual interests to those of the state. Yet prominent Athenians still voiced liberal ideas. The military general and orator **[2] Pericles** (495–429 BC), for example, said that laws should give equal justice to all, despite their differences. He called for toleration towards neighbours. And he pointed out the benefits of free trade and free movement: 'We throw open our city to the world, and never by alien acts exclude foreigners from any opportunity of learning or observing, although the eyes of an enemy may occasionally profit by our liberality'. But this equality, toleration and openness did not undermine Athens, he believed; rather, they enhanced its greatness.

Back in China, the influential philosopher **[3] Zhuang Zhou** or Zhuangzi (369–286 BC) argued that our knowledge was limited and our values were personal. Modern liberals see these as important reasons why authorities should not presume to interfere in people's lives. Zhuang Zhou agreed: the world, he said 'does not need governing; in fact it should not be governed'.

In India too, the emperor **[4] Ashoka the Great** (304–232 BC) called for freedom, responsibility, and political and religious tolerance. He perhaps saw this as a way of easing the tension between the many groups (Brahmans, Sramanas, Kshatriya) and ideas (Buddhism, Jainism, Ājīvikism) that comprised his complex society – arguing that mutual respect and peace was better than war.

Medieval ideas of freedom

In England, from around the fifth century onwards, the Anglo-Saxons had a well-developed system of property tenure. Monarchy was restrained too: some kings were appointed by the Witan, a council of nobles, which also set limits on their powers. Though these rights and restraints were swept away by the invading Normans in 1066, they resurfaced in 1215 in *Magna Carta*, the 'great charter' that outlined important principles of property rights and justice. Later kings sought to reassert their own power, but in the seventeenth century, **Sir Edward Coke** revived the *Magna Carta* principles – which still resonate in the English-speaking world today.

In Italy, the Dominican friar **[5] Thomas Aquinas** (1225–1274) expounded the idea of *natural law*. All beings must be true to their nature, he believed. Since humans are rational beings, that means using our reason to discover our natural purpose, and how best to achieve it. This in turn implies that we must be free to think. **Ayn Rand** would develop these ideas seven centuries later.

In the Middle East and beyond, Islam – from its earliest origins in the seventh century – was open to economic freedom and enterprise long before such values were respected in the West. Medieval Turkish emperors were often more tolerant than European monarchs of the same period. The Islamic scholar and jurist **[6] Ibn Khaldun** (1332–1406) understood how exploitation, by governments or others, was a huge disincentive against work, saving and progress:

Attacks on people's property remove the incentive to acquire and gain property. People then conclude that the only result of acquiring property is for it to be taken away again. When the incentive to acquire property is gone, people no longer make efforts to acquire it. The extent and degree to which property rights are infringed upon determines the extent and degree to which the efforts of the subjects to acquire property slacken.

In Spain, the *School of Salamanca*, originating from the work of **[7] Francisco de Vitoria** (1486–1546), attempted to apply the ideas of earlier clerics to the realities of the unfolding social, political and economic Renaissance. In doing so, these *scholastics*, as they were known, outlined a general liberal framework. The Spanish Jesuit priest **[8] Francisco Suárez** (1548–1617), for example, further developed the idea of natural law and argued that it implied *natural rights* to life, liberty, property and freedom of thought.

He also argued for limited government. As social creatures, he explained, we see the benefits of working for common purposes. So we form a political state, giving decision-making power to some kingly authority. But since that kingly power comes from the people, the people have the right to depose tyrannical monarchs. This early *social contract* idea influenced later liberal thinkers such as **John Locke** and **Hugo Grotius**.

The scholastic movement flourished for two centuries. Later members focused on *economic* liberties. They defended private ownership on the grounds that private owners took better care of property, which benefited the whole society. They also argued that the price of a good depended not on the cost of creating it, but on the demand for it – 'the common estimation' as one put it. The scholastics were more sympathetic to borrowing and interest than earlier clerics, recognising that credit now financed investment (and not just consumption), and that interest rates reflected the risk and opportunity cost faced by lenders.

Meanwhile, **[9] Akbar I** (1542–1605), the Muslim ruler of the Mughal Empire, was making liberal observations on tolerance – and extending it to Hindus and Jesuits, even as the Inquisition persecuted religious dissidents in Europe.

Liberal ideas, it seems, know no borders.

4 EARLY MODERN THINKERS

England in the sixteenth and seventeenth centuries was an unlikely location for an upsurge of liberalism. Religious disputes, dynastic conflicts and foreign wars left Tudor monarchs with little feeling for traditional English liberties. The Stuarts who succeeded them in 1603 had even less: being Scots, they did not share England's common law tradition; they spoke French at court, absorbing continental ideas on the absolute supremacy of kings. They did still have to ask Parliament for money to finance their spending, which put some limits on their absolutism. But Charles I (1600–1649) sought to circumvent this by imposing customs duties, raising forced loans (and jailing those who refused to pay), suspending Parliament, resurrecting feudal taxes, selling monopolies and imposing fines for breaches of long-forgotten laws.

Though Parliament was eventually reconvened, Charles's failed attempt to arrest five MPs was the last straw. A bloody civil war between Parliamentarian and Royalist factions ended with Charles's capture, trial and execution. But the new 'Lord Protector', Oliver Cromwell (1599–1658), proved no less tyrannical. In 1660 the monarchy was restored; but tensions continued between Parliament and Charles II

(1630–1685) and his successor James II (1633–1701), who eventually was deposed and fled. In a bloodless coup, known as the Glorious Revolution, Parliament invited the relatively liberal Dutch leader William, Prince of Orange (1650–1702), and his wife, James's daughter Mary (1662–1694) to be joint sovereigns. But they had to agree to a new constitutional contract, the 1689 *Bill of Rights*.

Such accidents of political history forced political theorists to reconsider the entire basis of constitutional government, the rights of individuals and the circumstances in which citizens might throw off a tyranny.

[10] Sir Edward Coke (1552–1634): English barrister, judge and politician. **Key ideas:** Limits to kingly power; rights of Parliament; no arbitrary taxes; rights of accused persons; independence of the judiciary; contract law.
Key works: *Remonstrance to the King* (1621); *Petition of Right* (1628).

Norfolk born and Cambridge educated, Coke (pronounced 'Cook') rose through the legal profession to become Attorney General under Elizabeth I and Chief Justice of the King's Bench under her successor, James I. Yet he quarrelled with both – and with James's successor, Charles I.

Coke's dispute with Elizabeth I was over the 'patents' and monopolies granted by the Crown. Initially justified as protecting industry, they had become ways of rewarding favourites and raising revenue; and English monarchs had extended them even to everyday products such as salt. Led by Coke, Parliament in 1601 brought monopolies under the authority of the courts. James I, however, rejected this curb on royal power and continued to grant these favours. Coke wrote Parliament's response, *Remonstrance to the King* (1621), asserting the rights of Parliament as the 'ancient and undoubted birthright and inheritance of the subjects of England'.

When Charles I jailed landowners who refused to pay forced loans or billet his soldiers in their homes, Parliament again objected. Coke famously declared: 'The house of every one is to him as his castle and fortress, as well for his defence against injury and violence as for his repose'. Or as it is paraphrased today, 'An Englishman's home is his castle'.

Coke drafted the *Resolutions* in which Parliament declared that the principles of *Magna Carta* still protected citizens against arbitrary detention and taxes levied without parliamentary consent. He led the writing of the *Petition of Right* (1628), spelling out the rights and liberties of citizens and paving the way for *Habeas Corpus*. Coke was also instrumental in creating the right to silence of accused persons, developing contract law and establishing the independence of the judiciary.

[11] Hugo Grotius (1583–1645): Dutch jurist and political philosopher. **Key ideas:** Rights over one's person and property. **Key work:** *On the Law of War and Peace* (1625).

In the Netherlands, another jurist was also thinking about the nature of rights. Hugo Grotius was a philosopher who held many illiberal views but made useful contributions to the liberal tradition. In particular, he maintained that individuals – and groups – possessed God-given *rights*, including the right to self-preservation and rights over property. We can therefore legitimately defend ourselves, and our property, from attack by others – even the state. Grotius also explained how our rights impose *duties* on others.

Yet he did not regard rights as inviolable. He saw situations in which they would have to be surrendered (perhaps forcibly). And since rights were a possession of the individual, they could be traded: people could sell themselves into slavery. Though later liberal theorists would denounce this latter point as self-contradictory, the idea that rights could be traded did inform **John Locke**'s view that state authority comes only from the rights that have been willingly given up by individual citizens.

[12] Thomas Hobbes (1588–1679): English political philosopher. **Key ideas:** Right of self-protection; practicality of a free society; social contract theory; government created by individuals to protect their rights; limits on government; right to overthrow bad government. **Key work:** *Leviathan* (1651).

Hobbes was even less of a liberal than **Hugo Grotius** – his ideal society featured an all-powerful sovereign – but parts of his thinking informed later liberal theory. He argued, for example, that curbs on liberty must be *justified*. He maintained that individuals have a 'right of nature' to defend themselves, even against the state. His view that free people could be self-governing stimulated liberals such as **Adam Smith** and **F. A. Hayek** to think about spontaneous social orders.

Perhaps most importantly, Hobbes's *social contract* reasoning became a vital tool for subsequent classical liberal thinkers such as **John Locke**. Human beings, he explained, are self-interested. With everyone out for themselves, the natural condition of humanity in the 'state of nature' would be a war of all against all. Life would be 'solitary, poor, nasty, brutish and short'. Simple self-preservation would make it rational for people to agree to mutual self-restraint.

But agreements can be broken, so the social contract must also provide for some governmental power to settle disputes. Hobbes thought this *sovereign* should be the sole lawgiver and administrator, the religious and educational authority, and would be empowered to order subjects to do anything short of self-injury.

Despite his absolutist conclusion, Hobbes set out some important liberal ideas. First, he saw government as created by free individuals: it could not legitimately be imposed on them. Second, individuals create government by transferring part of their authority to it. Third, government does not exist for its own purposes: it is created solely to protect and expand the freedom of the individuals who create it. Fourth, government has only limited authority – it cannot make those individuals kill or injure themselves. Fifth, its authority lasts only as long as it can protect and expand the freedom of its citizens: if it does not, they are under no obligation to obey it.

Such ideas – very modern departures in Hobbes's time – provided important material for subsequent liberal thinkers and helped create the intellectual background behind the Glorious Revolution and the American Revolution.

[13] John Milton (1608–1674): English poet, polemicist and statesman. **Key ideas:** Religious toleration, free speech and conscience; government as an implied contract. **Key works:** *The Doctrine and Discipline of Divorce* (1643); *Areopagitica* (1644); *A Treatise of Civil Power* (1659).

Best known for his religious epic *Paradise Lost* (1667), Milton also argued for the legality and morality of divorce, religious toleration and setting the church free from the political authorities. He stressed the political equality of individuals and saw government as an implied contract between rulers and the people.

Milton advocated free speech and freedom of conscience (at least among Protestants), believing that people can distinguish right from wrong if they can hear the competing arguments in open debate. 'Give me the liberty to know, to utter, and to argue freely', he wrote, 'according to conscience above all liberties'.

After the execution of Charles I in 1649, Milton became a polemicist for the incoming republican government of Oliver Cromwell. But he soon became an open critic of the autocratic Cromwell, urging him to respect his regime's implied contract with the people. Though no democrat, he dreamt of creating a more liberal republic (a 'free commonwealth'); but in fact the monarchy was restored.

[14] John Lilburne (1614–1657) and **[15] Richard Overton** (c.1599–1664): English civil rights activists ('Levellers'). **Key ideas:** Natural rights of life, liberty and property; rights of accused persons; religious tolerance; equality before the law; democracy; government subject to the people. **Key works:** *England's New Chains Discovered* (Lilburne, 1649); *An Arrow Against All Tyrants* (Overton, 1646).

John Lilburne's remarkable career sparked national debates on justice and authority. He argued for the right of accused persons to know the charges against them, to face their accusers and to avoid incriminating themselves. Governments of the time denied these rights, but that was not within their power, he asserted. People were born with such rights. Hence his nickname 'Freeborn John'.

Lilburne was dubbed a *Leveller* – not because he advocated financial equality but because he insisted that individuals were morally, politically and legally equal. The Levellers grew into an important reform movement, advocating religious tolerance, equality before the law, wider democracy and government subject to the will of the people.

Lilburne often flouted the official censorship that aimed to suppress radical ideas like his. Brought before the Star Chamber (the secretive court that crushed dissent), Lilburne refused to bow, maintaining that he and the judges were equals; he demanded to know the accusation against him and refused to swear an oath that might bind him to incriminate himself. For these contempts he was fined, whipped and pilloried. Even in the pillory, however, he lambasted his accusers and distributed more pamphlets to the crowd, leading to a further three years' imprisonment.

During the English Civil War, Lilburne joined the revolutionary forces, but was summoned before Parliament for attacking their religious intolerance. He went unpunished, but was soon jailed again for denouncing the luxury of MPs. Later, he was banished for calling a parliamentary committee 'unjust and unworthy men ... deserving worse than to be hanged'. On his unauthorised return to England he was promptly arrested, and spent another two years in prison.

Richard Overton, Lilburne's fellow Leveller, likewise argued for rights that were not taken for granted in his time: religious liberty, self-ownership and the natural rights of life, liberty and property. His attacks on the bishops, his blasphemous view that the immortal soul was 'a mere fiction', his liberal views on divorce, and his publication of unlicensed tracts, saw him too brought before Parliament. Rejecting Parliament's jurisdiction over such issues, he was jailed – but was released a year later, following public campaigns to free him.

Two years later, Overton, Lilburne and others were arrested over a pamphlet attacking Cromwell's despotism and branding him the 'new King'. The case did not succeed, but they were arrested again over rumours they were plotting a coup. When the monarchy was eventually restored, Overton remained true to his principles – being jailed yet again for a pamphlet attacking the new government.

[16] Algernon Sidney (1622–1683): English politician and republican theorist. **Key ideas:** Government exists for justice and liberty; right to resist tyrannical government and laws. **Key work:** *Discourses Concerning Government* (1698).

Sidney believed that government was necessary, but its role was limited to 'that which is most conducing to the establishment of justice and liberty'. 'Free men', he wrote, 'always have the right to resist tyrannical government'. Such ideas made him hugely influential in both Britain and America, even more so than **John Locke**. He was widely quoted by the critics of the Stuart monarchy, and inspired **John Trenchard** and **Thomas Gordon**, whose *Cato's Letters* roused the American revolutionaries. **Thomas Jefferson** proclaimed Sidney one of the main architects of American liberty.

Governments, to Sidney, were not above the law: 'That which is not just, is not law', he wrote in *Discourses Concerning Government* (1698), 'and that which is not law, ought not to be obeyed'. Sidney regarded absolute power as an evil, believing that citizens were entitled to a say in their government. In this he rose above faction. A republican, he sat at the trial of Charles I, but opposed the king's execution as vindictive and pointless. Later, when Cromwell sent troops to dissolve Parliament (for promoting reforms that Cromwell disliked), Sidney refused to leave his seat until ejected by force. Later still, when the monarchy was restored, he plotted the assassination of Charles II, whom he regarded as another tyrant. For this, he was tried for treason. Although there was only one witness against him (the law required two), the court, led by the infamous 'hanging judge' George Jeffreys (1645–1689), accepted the *Discourses* as a second 'witness' and Sidney was sent for execution. He continued to insist that all his life's actions were intended to 'uphold the common rights of mankind [and] the laws of this land ... against corrupt principles [and] arbitrary power...'

[17] John Locke (1632–1704): English philosopher, physician and activist. **Key ideas:** Limits to human knowledge; natural rights to life and liberty; contractual nature of government; government powers derive from individuals; property in one's own person; right to overthrow tyranny. **Key works:** *Letter Concerning Toleration* (1689); *Two Treatises of Government* (1690).

John Locke was one of the leading philosophers of the seventeenth century. His *Essay Concerning Human Understanding* (1689) stressed the limits of our knowledge about the natural and human worlds. But it is his *Letter Concerning Toleration* (1689) and *Two Treatises of Government* (1690) that secure his place as the father of 'classical' liberalism. They contain powerful arguments for the priority of the individual and for limits on government.

Locke was the son of a country lawyer, but thanks to the patronage of the local MP, he was able to attend Westminster School and Christ Church College, Oxford. After graduating, he taught Greek and rhetoric, then turned to science and medicine, becoming friends with Robert Boyle (1627–1691), Isaac Newton (1642–1726), Christiaan Huygens (1629–1695) and other prominent scientists.

He obtained government posts under Lord Shaftesbury (1621–1683), for whom he drafted *The Fundamental Constitution of the Carolinas* (and whose life he saved by removing an infected cyst on the liver). But Shaftesbury's hostility to James II led to him and Locke fleeing into exile. During his years in Holland and France, Locke wrote texts on toleration, plus his *Essay Concerning Human Understanding*. When James, mired in religious and political controversy, was deposed in favour of William and Mary, Shaftesbury and Locke returned, on the royal barge.

Locke then published, anonymously, his *Two Treatises of Government* (1690), justifying the overthrow of James II, scorning the 'divine right' of kings and asserting that legitimate government was based on a contract with the people, not on force and violence. His argument hinged on *natural rights* that were *prior* to government and to the *social contract* that created it.

Like **Thomas Hobbes**, Locke imagined a *state of nature* where there was no government. It would be a state of political equality, he maintained, with no one being politically superior or inferior to any other. Since we were God's creatures and property, others could not own or command us: there was no subordination between human beings. And having created us, God plainly wished us to survive: so we had no right to harm or kill ourselves, or others. On the contrary, we each had God-given natural rights to life, health and liberty.

But this *law of nature* could be violated, like the laws of human beings. In the state of nature, there would be no police, courts or judges, so we would all face the threat of violence and coercion. We might fight back, but injured parties tend to respond disproportionately. So we would find it preferable, Locke argued, to agree on some common system of justice.

Property could also lead to problems in the state of nature. Property itself was not illegitimate: God gave us the earth in common, but we could still acquire natural resources as our own. We own property in our own person, and when we mix our labour with a natural resource (by farming a piece of land, for example), that resource becomes ours, since the personal property that is our labour cannot be separated out from it. But there are limits. We have no right to acquire land and property that we cannot make use of. And an expanding population, the scarcity of resources, and people heaping up property through trade could lead to envy and disorder.

We create government, said Locke, to solve these 'state of nature' problems. We agree to *transfer* some parts of our rights to the state, lending it the authority to protect and preserve our rights to life, liberty, health and property, and to punish those who violate them. 'The only way whereby anyone divests himself of his natural liberty', he wrote, 'is by agreeing with other men to join and unite into a community, for their comfortable, safe and peaceable living one amongst another'. For this government to be legitimate, therefore, our individual authority must be transferred by *consent*, not force. But this *social contract* then becomes binding on us: we must accept that a legitimate government may suspend our own rights (by imprisonment, for example) if we violate the rights of others.

Such great power makes it crucial how laws are decided. Since everyone was a voluntary partner to the social contract, said Locke, everyone must be involved in the process. *Democracy* was therefore an essential part of the social contract, and legitimate government was subject to majority rule. By contrast, a government that was not curbed by the will of its citizens would become predatory and violate their rights. The citizens of such an *illegitimate* government were therefore perfectly justified in rebelling against it and overthrowing it, just as they might kill a predatory beast for their own protection:

> [W]henever the legislators endeavor to take away, and destroy the property of the people, or to reduce them to slavery under arbitrary power, they put themselves into a state of war with the people, who are thereupon absolved from any further obedience, and are left to the common refuge, which God hath provided for all men, against force and violence.

Such ideas were seized on by those who sought to justify the overthrow of James II, and strongly influenced the revolutions in America and France.

[18] Samuel von Pufendorf (1632–1694): German political philosopher, jurist and historian. **Key ideas:** Sociality as the basis of natural law; rights of justice and property make central authority unnecessary. **Key work:** *Of the Laws of Nature and Peoples* (1672).

Pufendorf's major works on natural law and the social contract influenced **John Locke** and **Montesquieu** and America's Founding Fathers.

Pufendorf took issue with **Thomas Hobbes** on two fronts. First, he argued that the supposed 'state of nature' would *not* be a state of war because humans possess a certain amount of natural 'sociality' that restrains them. He saw this sociality as the basis of natural law. But it would be an insecure peace, and we would need to *strengthen* our sociality to maintain it.

Second, Pufendorf argued that the state that we create in order to bolster this uneasy peace is not a leviathan with a body and mind of its own. If we are to live in peace and harmony with others, we do not need a strong central authority, but interpersonal rights, rules of just conduct and property. The 'will of the state' is no more than the wills of the individuals who comprise it.

[19] William Wollaston (1659–1724): English theologian and philosopher. **Key ideas:** The principles of property rights; the right to life; the right to the pursuit of happiness. **Key work:** *The Religion of Nature Delineated* (1722).

Staffordshire born and Cambridge educated, Wollaston became a Birmingham cleric; but an inheritance allowed him to spend time in the study of philosophy, history and religion. He became very influential: his book *The Religion of Nature Delineated* (1722) sold 10,000 copies. His stress on the right to life and the 'pursuit of happiness' had an impact on **Benjamin Franklin** and is reflected in the American Declaration of Independence.

People's lives and bodies, argued Wollaston, are part of their individuality, and are their sole property. Strength and power does not justify anyone taking them: might and right are different things. But reason is universal: whatever you deem acceptable for others, you must accept for yourself too. On the same logic, nobody can 'interrupt the happiness' of another: indeed, people have the right to defend themselves from attacks on their life, property and happiness.

Wollaston also set out the core principles of property rights: *exclusivity*, *transferability* and *enforceability*. Ownership, he said, implies the 'sole right of using and disposing' of something. Property may be transferred by 'compact or donation'. It was unjust to 'usurp or invade the property of another'. And victims had the right to recover what is stolen from them – or its equivalent value.

[20] John Trenchard (1662–1723) and **[21] Thomas Gordon** (c.1691–1750): English authors and reformers. **Key ideas:** Application of the principles of natural rights and consensual government to contemporary government; inspiration of American revolutionaries. **Key work:** *Cato's Letters* (1720–1723).

Between 1720 and 1723, Trenchard and Gordon co-authored *Cato's Letters*, a series of 138 newspaper essays, named after the staunch republican critic of Julius Caesar. The essays became hugely popular for their scathing views on contemporary issues and intelligent discussion of liberal ideas.

Trenchard, a wealthy reformer, first collaborated with the witty and articulate Gordon on *The Independent Whig*, a weekly that denounced Catholic efforts to return the Stuarts to the throne, and argued that freedom of conscience was an inalienable natural right that neither clerics nor politicians could extinguish.

Following **Algernon Sidney**, *Cato's Letters* slammed the corruption and tyranny of big-government politicians and officials, and used **John Locke**'s theories of natural law and natural rights to call for freedom of speech. They attributed the 1720 financial crash (set off when politicians granted the South Sea Company a monopoly on South American trade that subsequently proved worthless) to a bloated and interventionist government that fed the dishonesty and corruption of politicians, ministers and royals. Their assertion that government rested on consent, and of the public's right to throw off tyranny, made the *Letters* (and the ideas of Sidney and Locke) particularly popular in America.

5   THE AGE OF REASON

The 1746 defeat of Charles Edward Stuart ('Bonnie Prince Charlie') ended the prospect of a return to French-style absolutism, and secured Britain's new constitutional monarchy. Scotland, in particular, benefited from the new stability and the opening up of trade following the 1707 Act of Union. In what was called the Scottish Enlightenment, a new wave of Scottish thinkers such as **David Hume** and **Adam Smith** explored exciting new ideas on the workings of society, on ethics, on economics and taxation, on political structures and the limits to government power, and on the rights and freedoms of individuals. Even in France, as these ideas spread, there was greater questioning of the power and authority of the Catholic Church, and more non-aristocrats were being appointed to government on the basis of merit.

English and French liberalism both sought to base government on rational principles, but developed in quite different ways. English liberalism focused on the rights of ordinary people against Continental-style absolutist power, stressing individualism and a minimal state. French liberalism, by contrast, accepted the prevailing legal, social and religious institutions, but stressed the role that democracy could play in making the state work more rationally. Being thus democratic but statist, French liberalism was often associated with the Left, as embodied in the political philosopher Jean-Jacques Rousseau (1712–1778) – though this consensus was later shaken by the more Lockean liberalism of **Voltaire**, **Montesquieu** and **Benjamin Constant**.

[22] Bernard Mandeville (1670–1733): Anglo-Dutch physician, moral philosopher, political theorist and satirist. **Key ideas:** Self-interest as the basis of a functioning society; division of labour; altruism's destructive effect on incentives. **Key works:** *The Grumbling Hive, or Knaves Turn'd Honest* (1705); *The Fable of the Bees* (1714).

Born in Rotterdam, Mandeville spent most of his life in England. He argued – shockingly – that society rested on self-interest rather than benevolence. He expressed this idea in the doggerel poem *The Grumbling Hive, or Knaves Turn'd Honest* (1705). This scandalous but witty satire on the state of England was republished in 1714 as *The Fable of the Bees*, with additional essays on moral and social theory.

Mandeville's verses imagined a thriving bee community 'blest with content and honesty' – until the bees are suddenly made altruistic. Then, without personal gain and ambition to drive them, they become idle and impoverished. His point, elaborated more academically by **Adam Smith**, was that self-interest, if properly channelled, prompted innovation and effort and therefore progress – though Smith disagreed with Mandeville's view that self-sacrifice was harmful. Our supposedly 'vicious' traits, such as greed, were central to our welfare, argued Mandeville. A politician who tried to curb 'vice' or promote 'virtue' would disrupt the workings of society. But by channelling greed, 'Private vices ... may be turned into publick benefits'.

In *A Search into the Nature of Society* (1723), Mandeville rejected the prevailing theories that our morality came through self-denial, a 'moral sense', or reason. Rather, it grew out of our desire to protect ourselves when faced with the 'evil' of other people's self-serving actions. Ironically, therefore, 'Evil ... is the grand principle that makes us social creatures ... the moment evil ceases, the society must be spoiled, if not totally dissolved'.

Underneath this impishly provocative language, as **F. A. Hayek** pointed out 250 years later, is a hugely important principle of liberal theory: that complex societies evolve out of the everyday interactions of individuals who are motivated by self-interest. When we try to make people behave differently, we risk tearing this complex web of action.

[23] Montesquieu [Charles-Louis de Secondat, Baron de La Brède et de Montesquieu] (1689–1755): French lawyer and political philosopher. **Key ideas:** Constitutional theory; the division of powers; due process of law; the principles of justice; presumption of innocence; free trade as a restraint on governments. **Key works:** *Persian Letters* (1721); *The Spirit of the Laws* (1748).

Montesquieu's highly original thinking on the relationship between freedom and law, and his innovative constitutional system based on the *separation of powers*, made his books *Persian Letters* (1721) and *The Spirit of the Laws* (1748) particularly influential in France and America, where they provided a vision for post-revolutionary government.

Montesquieu saw the key political problem as how to contain the power of state authorities and prevent a slide into tyranny. Building on **John Locke**'s *Second Treatise*, he argued for the division of powers, such that 'power should be a check to power'. Legislative, executive and judicial authority should be held by different bodies, so that abuses by one branch could be restrained by the others. The legislature would have the power to tax, which would curb the executive. The executive would be able to veto decisions of the legislature. The legislature itself would be divided into two houses, so that one could block decisions from the other. The judiciary would be independent but limited to ensuring that the laws were applied without favour. There should be due process of law, including the right to a fair trial, the presumption of innocence and punishments that fit the crime.

Montesquieu was impressed at how Britain had curbed its monarchy. But he thought that governments needed little power anyway, their role being to leave us as free as possible while protecting us from harm. The law should therefore address only public order and security, and strive to maximise freedom. It had no business in areas such as religion or lifestyle. It should address only people's practical actions, not their supposed motives. And laws should be known, general and predictable, not arbitrary, personal and capricious.

Like **Adam Smith** after him, Montesquieu lambasted government interference in commerce (especially foreign trade), arguing that exchange benefits both sides, not just the seller. Unlike war and conquest, international trade brought its benefits without the need for armies or expense. It also limited the power of governments: international markets were impossible for individual states to control; exchange rates were set by the merchants of many countries, not by any country's decree; since commerce enriches us, governments had an incentive to facilitate it rather than impede it; and the need for trading countries to remain creditworthy helped curb budget irresponsibility. Economic reality was therefore a useful restraint on the vaulting ambitions of politicians.

[24] Voltaire [François-Marie Arouet] (1694–1778): French playwright, novelist and polemicist. **Key ideas:** Criticism of aristocracy and church corruption; role of reason and freedom in moral action; tolerance and free speech; rule of law; criticism of mercantilism; utility of property rights. **Key work:** *Philosophical Letters on the English* (1734).

Voltaire was an important figure in the French Enlightenment. He upset the mighty with his polemics on the injustices of his time, and on the hypocrisy and corruption of politicians and clerics. As he famously observed, 'In general, the art of government consists in taking as much money as possible from one party of the citizenry to give to the other'.

Accused of defamation and threatened by a powerful aristocrat, he went into exile in England, where he met key intellectuals and reformers, and became familiar with the work of **John Locke**. Like **Montesquieu**, he was attracted to Britain's liberal institutions, civil liberties, constitutional government and freedom of speech. He decided to spend his career promoting freedom, tolerance, free speech and free trade. His *Philosophical Letters on the English* (1734) urged France to overthrow aristocratic powers, and criticised the intolerance of the Church. A spell in the Bastille did not stop his attacks on the injustice and repression then rife in continental Europe.

Voltaire campaigned for a constitutional monarchy in France. He thought the shortsightedness of the masses made democracy unreliable, but believed that an enlightened monarch could make reforms that would improve the welfare of the whole population. He argued for liberty, asserting that although human beings were governed by natural laws, they had free will. Moral action came through reason and the freedom to act upon it, and free speech was a vital part of this. He never actually said 'I disagree with what you say, but I will defend to the death your right to say it'. But the phrase aptly summarises his views.

Voltaire sought to limit arbitrary power by bringing it under the rule of law. He argued for toleration, saying that the state should not promote particular doctrines such as Christianity. He asserted the right to a fair trial and for careers to be open to everyone, and called for a fairer tax system. He criticised mercantilism, saying that wealth did not exist in a country's gold and silver, but in the hard work, productivity and skill of its workers – ideas that **Adam Smith** would develop. And he understood the power of motivation: he defended private property, not from a natural law viewpoint as **John Locke** had done, but because it gave people the best incentive to strive for self-improvement.

[25] François Quesnay (1694–1774): French surgeon and founder of the Physiocrat School of economics. **Key ideas:** Critique of mercantilism; social harmony through freedom; deregulation and free trade. **Key work:** *Economic Table* (1758).

In contrast to the prevailing *mercantilism* – which regarded the wealth of a nation in terms of its stockpiles of gold and silver and its ability, through exporting, to add to them – the French 'Physiocrat' economists, led by Quesnay and **Turgot**, argued that the foundation of national wealth was productive work.

These ideas greatly influenced **Adam Smith**'s critique of mercantilism in *The Wealth of Nations*. But Quesnay – living as he did in a highly agricultural economy – argued that only farm labour was truly productive, and that other work, such as that of artisans, merchants, landlords and capital providers, merely supported it. Smith, with a more sophisticated view of commerce, recognised that any form of useful production contributed to the national wealth.

Quesnay maintained that social harmony was best achieved through laissez-faire policy and open competition. Accordingly, he called for an end to ancient restrictions on agricultural production. He also argued that the mercantilist policy of raising tariffs and barriers against imported goods in fact deepened poverty, and called for Louis XV (1710–1774) – to whose influential mistress, Madame de Pompadour, he was physician – to end such protectionism.

[26] Benjamin Franklin (1706–1790): American states-man and polymath. **Key ideas:** Drafting the American Declaration of Independence and Constitution; natural rights; monetary prudence; trade and peace. **Key work:** *Poor Richard's Almanack* (1732–1758).

Franklin was a senior figure in the creation of the United States: he was 70 when he helped draft the Declaration of Independence, and later he helped draft the Constitution. His signature appears on both.

Some regard Franklin as a conservative, though his ad-vocacy of independence and his pithy writings on liberty earn him a place among liberal thinkers. Despite the dangers of revolution, he urged that liberty must be defended at any cost, saying, 'Those who would give up essential Liberty, to purchase a little temporary Safety, deserve neither Liberty nor Safety'.

Franklin was certainly a religious liberal: raised as a Puritan, he remained a believer, but came to reject all organised religion. (For example, he never went through a church marriage with his long-term partner.) And he promoted the natural rights hypothesis of **John Locke**: 'Freedom is not a gift bestowed upon us by other men', he wrote, 'but a right that belongs to us by the laws of God and nature'.

Franklin advanced such views through the newspapers and almanacs that he published and which made him wealthy. He also made money printing laws and banknotes, but warned against a surfeit of either, writing: 'Paper money in moderate quantities has been found beneficial; when more than the occasions of commerce require, it depreciated and is mischievous, and the populace are apt to demand more than is necessary'. It was a point that **Milton Friedman** would revive two centuries later.

Franklin spent many years in Europe, as agent for Pennsylvania and then as his new country's ambassador to France. There he grew familiar with the Physiocrat ideas of **Quesnay** and **Turgot**, which saw economic growth as built on commerce, competition and free trade. Franklin summed up the policy concisely: 'The system of America is universal commerce with every nation; war with none'.

[27] David Hume (1711–1776): Scottish philosopher and historian. **Key ideas:** Society based on utility, not reason; property rights; limited government. **Key work:** *Essays, Moral, Political, and Literary* (1742).

David Hume's insights into human understanding, causation, necessity, morality, justice, economics, political theory and religion make him one of the most important philosophers of all time. He also influenced and inspired key liberal thinkers, from his friend **Adam Smith**, through **Immanuel Kant** (who remarked that Hume woke him from his 'dogmatic slumbers'), to **F. A. Hayek**.

Hume was radical in defying the philosophical conventions of the time with his sceptical, empirical method; but he reached the more conservative conclusion that peace, prosperity and justice are best served by following conventional rules.

Hume entered Edinburgh University at the age of ten or eleven. At just 23, he began his monumental *Treatise of Human Nature* (1739). Though denied academic posts because of his scandalous religious scepticism, after his *Enquiry Concerning Human Understanding* (1748) he was asked to be Librarian at the Faculty of Advocates. There, he began his bestselling *History of England* (1754–62), which made his fame and fortune. In 1763 he became private secretary to the British Ambassador in Paris, where his famously engaging manner brought him numerous salon invitations. He remained a lifelong atheist, but ensured that his most shockingly sceptical work, *Dialogues Concerning Natural Religion* (1779), was published only posthumously.

Hume traced moral sentiments to the *sympathy* (today we would say *empathy*) that we have with other humans – a revolutionary idea which Smith developed in *The Theory of Moral Sentiments* (1759). Nature, said Hume, has given us useful *natural virtues* such as charity, kindness and parental love. But to capture the full benefits of living in today's large societies, we need more – *artificial virtues* such as respect for property rights, contracts and justice. We respect these virtues not from instinct but out of utility, because they enable us to avoid theft and violence, and to live peacefully together. Eventually they become so ingrained within our social practices that they become matters of habit. We do not require government to create this beneficial order: civil society can arise prior to government.

The specific rules that advanced these virtues were matters of convention. It did not matter so much what the exact rules of property or justice were, provided they worked tolerably well and were accepted. Thus, having a justice system that secured peace was more critical than the precise laws it was based on. For people to invest and create wealth, there must be known, accepted and functioning rules of ownership, transfer and contract – even though the exact rules may well differ between societies.

For Hume, the basis of a thriving social order was a functioning spontaneous order, shaped by general agreement and honed by experience. He rejected all *rationalist* explanations such as those of **John Locke**. Reason, he argued, may help us achieve our desires, but does not *motivate* us. Reason was merely 'the slave of the passions'.

One thing that reason and experience did teach us, however, was the need to limit government power: 'Political writers have established it as a maxim, that, in contriving any system of government, and fixing the several checks and controls of the constitution, every man ought to be supposed a knave, and to have no other end, in all his actions, than private interest'.

[28] Adam Ferguson (1723–1816): Scottish social theorist. **Key ideas:** Spontaneous order; division of labour; innovation and growth. **Key work:** *Essay on the History of Civil Society* (1767).

Ferguson is often called the 'father of modern sociology' on account of his *Essay on the History of Civil Society* (1767). He made few original contributions to liberal thought, but is remembered for his pithy phrase on spontaneous order: 'Every step and every movement of the multitude, even in what are termed enlightened ages, are made with equal blindness to the future; and nations stumble upon establishments, which are indeed the result of human action, but not the execution of any human design'.

He rejected the warlike *state of nature* idea of **Thomas Hobbes**, pointing out (like **Samuel von Pufendorf**) that human beings are naturally *social* creatures. Nobody ever existed in isolation: people are shaped by the family, language and moral norms they are born into – in short, by *society*.

Ferguson outlined the idea of the *division of labour*, which **Adam Smith** would later develop:

> The artist [artisan] finds, that the more he can confine his attention to a particular part of any work, his productions are the more perfect, and grow under his hands in the greater quantities. Every undertaker in manufacture finds, that the more he can subdivide the tasks of his workmen, and the more hands he can employ on separate articles, the more are his expenses diminished, and his profits increased.

Through self-interest, therefore, people unintentionally produced a world of creative diversity, efficiency and innovation, which fuelled growth and prosperity. But

Ferguson questioned whether the division of labour was entirely benign. It might, he thought, result in class stratification and social tensions – and, if security were left wholly up to a specialist military profession, to potential tyranny.

[29] Adam Smith (1723–1790): Scottish philosopher and economist. **Key ideas:** Human empathy and spontaneous order; attack on mercantilism; mutual gains from free trade; productivity; division of labour; the invisible hand; markets steer resources to productive uses; justice; limited government. **Key works:** *The Theory of Moral Sentiments* (1759); *The Wealth of Nations* (1776).

Adam Smith was one of the most prominent thinkers of the eighteenth-century Scottish Enlightenment. An avid collector of books and ideas, he wrote and lectured about ethics, jurisprudence, literature, politics and the philosophy of science. Today he is best remembered as a pioneering economist: his hugely influential *An Inquiry into the Nature and Causes of the Wealth of Nations* (1776) made the case for free markets, open competition and limited government.

Yet it was Smith's earlier book on ethics, *The Theory of Moral Sentiments* (1759), which brought him fame. Enlightenment philosophers sought a firmer foundation for ethics than the dogma handed down by clerics and rulers. Some searched for 'rational' alternatives. Smith, by contrast, suggested that morality was a feature of human social psychology. We have a natural *sympathy* (today we would say *empathy*) for others. Their pleasure or pain affects us; and we like to act in ways that earn their respect, not their wrath. As the book begins, 'How selfish soever man may be supposed, there are evidently some principles in his nature, which interest him in the fortune of others, and render their happiness necessary to him, though he derives nothing from it except the pleasure of seeing it'. This natural feeling for others leads us to consider how our actions affect others, and to restrain our selfishness such that an *impartial spectator* might approve. This restraint, observed Smith, helps produce a well-functioning social order, which then endures.

The book was an instant success. It prompted the Duke of Buccleuch's stepfather to hire Smith, on a lifetime income, to tutor the young duke and take him around Europe. In France and Switzerland, Smith was able to discuss ideas with the greatest European thinkers, and picked up endless facts about different systems of commerce and regulation. He started writing what would become *The Wealth of Nations*, weaving his own and others' ideas into a new, systematic and modern approach to economics.

The prevailing economic system in Smith's day was *mercantilism*, which measured a nation's wealth by its stockpiles of gold and silver. Policy was directed at swelling those stockpiles by selling as much as possible to other countries, and buying as little as possible from them. Imports were choked off by tariffs and regulations; exports were encouraged by subsidies.

Smith, however, pointed out that both sides benefit from trade, not just the sellers. The sellers get cash, certainly, but the buyers get goods that they value more than the money they pay. Neither side would enter into a bargain that did not benefit them. Smith concluded that what made a country rich was not its gold and silver, but its trade and commerce; and the measure of that was how much it actually produced and exchanged – the measure we today call *gross domestic product*. The way to increase that product, he argued, was to liberate commerce, not restrict it.

Indeed, we can increase our product further through the huge productivity gains made possible by specialisation – the *division of labour*. Using the example of a pin factory, Smith showed how dividing production into many specialist tasks can boost output thousands of times. Producers can then create far more than they need for their own consumption, and exchange their surplus with others, who in turn are skilled at other things. So everyone gains from the specialisation of others. Producers can also use some of their surplus to invest in capital goods, such as factories and tools, which raise their productivity – and national wealth – even more.

This is a hugely cooperative system, though nobody plans it that way. People produce and exchange goods to benefit themselves, not others: 'It is not from the benevolence of the butcher, the brewer or the baker that we expect our dinner, but from their regard to their own interest'. Yet without intending to, they also enrich and improve the lives of those they trade with, and ultimately the whole society:

> Every individual ... neither intends to promote the public interest, nor knows how much he is promoting it ... he

> intends only his own security; and by directing that
> industry in such a manner as its produce may be of the
> greatest value, he intends only his own gain, and he is in
> this, as in many other cases, led by an invisible hand to
> promote an end which was no part of his intention.

So widely beneficial is this unplanned cooperation, that it
embraces the whole known world: even a simple woollen
coat, explains Smith, contains the labour of thousands of
specialists from scores of countries – from shepherds to
spinners, dyers, sailors, toolmakers and retailers.

Another unplanned benefit of trade is that it automatically steers resources to where they are needed. Where
things are scarce, consumers are willing to pay more for
them; since there is more profit in supplying them, producers create more. When there is a glut, prices fall, and
producers switch their effort into producing things of
higher value. Industry thus remains focused on people's
most important needs. So, without any regulation and
planning:

> [T]he obvious and simple system of natural liberty es-
> tablishes itself of its own accord. Every man ... is left
> perfectly free to pursue his own interest in his own way
> ... The sovereign is completely discharged from a duty [for
> which] no human wisdom or knowledge could ever be
> sufficient; the duty of superintending the industry of pri-
> vate people, and of directing it towards the employments
> most suitable to the interest of the society.

But this is automatic only when there is free trade and competition. When governments grant subsidies or monopolies to favoured producers, or shelter them behind tariff walls, consumers are exploited. The poor suffer most, facing higher costs for the necessities that they rely on.

A justice system that protects property rights is vital too. If people are to build up capital, they must be confident that it will be secure. The countries that prosper are those with institutions that protect people's property from theft. This includes a subtle kind of theft – merchants using their political influence with legislators to win monopolies, tax preferences, controls and other privileges that distort markets in their favour – what today we call *crony capitalism*.

Smith therefore concluded that government must be limited. It has core functions such as defence, justice, infrastructure and education. But it should keep markets open and free, and not distort them. In any event, human beings are individuals with minds of their own, who thwart the authorities' plans:

> The man of system ... seems to imagine that he can arrange the different members of a great society with as much ease as the hand arranges the different pieces upon a chess-board. He does not consider that in the great chess-board of human society, every single piece has a principle of motion of its own, altogether different from that which the legislature might choose to impress upon it.

[30] Richard Price (1723–1791): Welsh nonconformist preacher, pamphleteer and radical. **Key ideas:** Rights of women; contractual basis of government; election reform; opposition to public debt. **Key works:** *Appeal to the Public on the Subject of the National Debt* (1772); *Observations on the Nature of Civil Liberty* (1776).

Price became famous for his defence of the American colonists in their dispute with Britain, but is best remembered today as the mentor of **Mary Wollstonecraft**, who developed his ideas on the rights of women.

A nonconformist preacher, Price argued that monarchs had no divine right to govern, but held power in trust from the people. The only legitimate monarchs were Britain's, who were bound by an explicit contract with the people, namely the 1689 Bill of Rights. He believed that the American revolutionaries (and later the French) were simply striving for the same kind of contract. Much of **Thomas Paine**'s *The Rights of Man* (1791) was based on his arguments; he became friends with **Benjamin Franklin** and John Adams (1735–1826), received an honorary degree from Yale and was offered (but declined) American citizenship. Regarding France, he corresponded with **Turgot** and supported the French revolutionaries, but died before the full horror of the Terror unfolded.

Price also argued for reform of Britain's notoriously corrupt parliamentary election system and against the slave trade. His 1771 attack on the existence of the national debt informed the decision of Prime Minister William Pitt (1759–1806), ten years later, to establish a sinking fund to reduce it.

[31] Immanuel Kant (1724–1804): German philosopher. **Key ideas:** Universal right to freedom; individuals as ends, not means; state limited to defending rights and freedom; moral action demands free choice; moral and political principles must be universal; rights are conventional, not natural; government as contractual and limited, not democratic; rule of law. **Key works:** *Critique of Pure Reason* (1781); *The Metaphysics of Morals* (1797).

Kant is remembered mostly for his views on metaphysics and the theory of knowledge, but he also explored ethics and political theory. He upheld freedom as a universal right, saw people as equal and independent, argued that individuals cannot be regarded as *means* to other people's ends, and sought to limit the state to defending rights and freedom. All this marks him as a liberal, though at other points he is conservative and authoritarian.

To Kant, the basis of morality was reason. But in order to use our reason, we must be free – free to put forward and argue our views, and free to act upon them. If we cannot control our own actions, they (and we) cannot be called moral or immoral. Moral law, he argued, is not hypothetical, like telling someone not to steal if they want to avoid punishment. It is a *categorical imperative*, a command from our reason that must be obeyed for its own sake, and at all times. Reason tells us that we should act only in ways that we are willing to see being applied as *universal law* for everyone.

Politics too should be based on universal principles. Kant accepted the need for government: society could function only if freedom (from which our other rights stem) was guaranteed by the state. But rights (including property rights) were things specified by the state, not a part of natural law. If there was any exception, it was freedom itself: '*Freedom* (independence from being constrained by another's choice) ... is the only original right belonging to every man by virtue of his humanity'.

Kant was one of the first to explore what a *Rechtstaat* or 'just state' would look like. It cannot be democratic, he argued, since majority rule threatens the liberty of minorities. Rather, it would be constitutional – contractual and limited by law, recognising the liberty and the equal civil and judicial rights of each person. The sovereign must obey the law too (though, unlike many liberals, Kant did not accept the right to revolt). And he argued for a tax-funded safety net, saying that the pressures on people suffering extreme need may prevent them from being responsible for their own actions. But beyond those guarantees, the state had no paternal responsibility to direct our actions: 'No one has a right to compel me to be happy in the peculiar way in which he may think of the well-being of other men', he wrote. But, 'everyone is entitled to seek his own happiness in the way that it seems to him best, if it does not infringe the liberty of others in striving for a similar end for themselves'.

[32] Turgot [Anne-Robert-Jacques Turgot, Baron de Laune] (1727–1781): French economist and statesman. **Key ideas:** Balanced budgets; deregulation; subjective theory of value. **Key work:** *Reflections on the Formation and Distribution of Wealth* (1769–70).

A friend of **Voltaire**, and influenced by Physiocrat ideas, Turgot became one of the most prominent liberals of his time. A gifted economist, in 1774 he became Controller-General of the national budget, where he cut the deficit and liberalised trade. As well as very original contributions in economics, he also wrote on the theory of progress.

Turgot was given the chance to implement his liberal ideas when appointed tax collector for Limoges. He abolished the *corvée* (unpaid labour on government projects), and financed roads and canals to aid commerce. As Controller-General, he promised Louis XVI 'no bankruptcy, no tax increases, no borrowing'. He abolished price controls on grain, arguing that local merchants were better judges of markets than distant officials – though a bad harvest led to price increases and consequent unrest. He deregulated business, halting the Hôtel-Dieu's monopoly privilege of selling meat on Friday, and ended the *corvée en nature* (unpaid work that people were obliged to do for aristocratic landowners). But such reforms created political enemies, and he lost his job after criticising France's large military spending.

On progress, Turgot wrote that we must make a thousand errors to find one truth, and that we need a deep knowledge of history to prevent further errors. He believed that self-interest was the prime mover of progress, and that in free markets, individual interest always coincided with the general interest. Like **Voltaire**, he believed in an enlightened constitutional monarchy. He supported a system of state schools to teach liberal principles and counter the Church schools' intolerance.

In economics, Turgot took on the ancient prejudice against 'usury' by pointing out that interest rates must reflect the scarcity or abundance of savings, the time needed for production, and the uncertainty of the result. Lenders were therefore not just idle funders but skilled and active entrepreneurs, seeking out profitable ventures and bearing the risks involved. It was in fact a capital market, with producers demanding funds to invest and capital owners eyeing the alternative uses for their savings (what today we call *opportunity cost*). High interest rates were not morally wrong, but simply the price of capital to the most risky and long-term ventures. Such market pressures efficiently steered savings towards useful projects.

A century and more later, the Austrian School economists such as **Carl Menger**, **Ludwig von Mises**, Friedrich von Wieser (1851–1926) and **F. A. Hayek** would develop these highly original ideas, along with Turgot's less developed ideas on marginal utility and the subjective value that people attach to objects. Turgot had a further impact as a teacher of **Nicolas de Condorcet**, who, after Turgot's fall, remained an outspoken advocate for his ideas on free trade, the abolition of forced labour and a free society.

[33] Anders Chydenius (1729–1803): Scandinavian politician and economist. **Key ideas:** Free trade; self-interest; free speech; deregulation. **Key work:** *The National Gain* (1765).

Born in Finland, then under Swedish control, Chydenius's 1765 pamphlet *Den Nationnale Winsten* (*The National Gain*) briefly outlined many of the ideas that **Adam Smith** would develop at length in *The Wealth of Nations* (1776). Like Smith he rejected mercantilist export subsidies as harmful, calling for free trade, commerce and industry. The guiding principle of economics, he argued, was freedom. People engaged in trade, and struck wage bargains, for reasons of self-interest. But they made gains only by producing what their neighbours valued – creating an economic gain for the whole nation: '[E]very individual spontaneously tries to find the place and the trade in which he can best increase the national gain, if laws do not prevent him from doing so'.

In other writings, Chydenius explored liberal ideas about the relation between the citizen and the state. He argued, a century before **John Stuart Mill**, that truth would emerge through the competition of ideas, making free speech a key foundation of understanding and progress.

As a parliamentarian and reformer, Chydenius was active in a campaign to ease trade restrictions on local merchants. He also promoted a law to abolish censorship, allow people to write freely about public affairs, and make government information freely available to the public.

[34] Joseph Priestley (1733–1804): English chemist, physicist, dissenter, reformer and liberal theorist.
Key ideas: Free speech; religious toleration; civil and political rights; anti-slavery. **Key work:** *Essay on the First Principles of Government* (1768).

Priestley is remembered today for his discovery of oxygen and his writings on electricity, but in his own times he was also known for his controversial liberal views. Influenced by **Richard Price**, he favoured free exchange of ideas, and argued for toleration and equal rights for Dissenters – religious groups that had broken away from the established Church. Dissenters (like Priestley himself) were officially barred from public office, the universities and the military. Though few were prosecuted, they still resented such discrimination.

In his *Essay on the First Principles of Government* (1768), Priestley made the distinction between *civil rights*, due naturally to everyone as members of human society, and *political rights*, granted to citizens as members of a polity. He argued that civil rights should be drawn as widely as possible. He also insisted that there were public and private spheres to our lives (an idea later elaborated by **F. A. Hayek**), and that government should be involved only in the public sphere. To Priestley, education and religion were firmly in the private sphere, being matters of individual conscience, and no business of the state.

Priestley applied his arguments against religious bigotry to call for toleration in other parts of life. He was active in several reform movements, exposing official corruption and supporting (like Price) parliamentary reform, the abolition of the slave trade and the American revolutionaries. But his controversial support of the French Revolution provoked violence against him, prompting him to emigrate and spend his last years in the US.

6   REVOLUTIONARIES AND RADICALS

By the mid 1700s, Britain's American colonists were grow-ing increasingly discontented at the way Britain was gov-erning them and regulating their trade. The 1765 Stamp Act (requiring that legal documents, newspapers and many other printed materials should be printed on London-made paper and bear a revenue stamp in English currency) pre-cipitated a crisis. It was seen as taxation without consent (or, in the popular phrase, *taxation without representation*). This flouted the ancient rights of the British people – of whom the colonists regarded themselves as part.

When the British government passed punitive legisla-tion and took up arms against them, the colonists came to see rebellion as entirely justified, taking their arguments from the British liberal philosophers who had wrestled with the events of the Civil War and the Glorious Revolu-tion. And they would draw on Magna Carta and the Bill of Rights in shaping their own new republic.

While the American Revolution may have cheered lib-erals, the French Revolution, a little later, divided opinion. At first, with the *Declaration of the Rights of Man and the Citizen*, things looked promising; but as different factions vied for power, one tyranny was merely replaced by a bloodier one. French liberals such as **Condorcet** and **Benjamin Constant** struggled to work out how such regimes had come about, and how to restrain them through constitutions. English liberals, along with many conservatives, sought to avoid France's turmoil by reforming the electoral system. German liberals such as **Wilhelm von Humboldt** began thinking about the role of a liberal state and the moral development of those who comprise it.

In this hothouse, radical ideas sprang up. **Jeremy Bentham** proposed a completely new moral system as the basis for public policy. **William Godwin** questioned whether governments were needed at all. Godwin's wife **Mary Wollstonecraft** argued (highly controversially at the time) that women should have the same rights as men. The world was changing: not just industrially, but socially and intellectually too.

[35] Thomas Paine (1737–1809): Anglo-American pamphleteer, journalist and polemicist. **Key ideas:** Case for the American Revolution; individualism; religious and racial toleration; moral equality; republican liberalism; civil society. **Key works:** *Common Sense* (1776); *The Rights of Man* (1791–92).

Born into a Quaker family in England, Paine emigrated to America (at the suggestion of **Benjamin Franklin**, whom he met in London) largely to escape debts and what he saw as persecution in England. He brought liberal ideas to a huge public through his popular books, pamphlets and journalism.

His *Common Sense* (1776) caught the revolutionary mood of America: around half a million copies were sold. It stated pithily his case against the illiberal actions of a corrupt British government, explained why independence was now inevitable, and bolstered confidence in the future of America as a just, democratic, liberal republic that would be an example to the world.

Later, in 1790, Paine visited revolutionary France, and found further success with *The Rights of Man* (1791–92), rebutting Edmund Burke's counter-revolutionary *Reflections on the Revolution in France* (1790) and lambasting corrupt monarchies and institutions. His new book sold a million copies and prompted the British authorities to charge him with sedition. He involved himself in French politics but became caught up in the factionalism of the times: he was imprisoned and only narrowly escaped execution.

Paine defended individualism and preached toleration (including coexistence with the indigenous American peoples) based on the moral equality of all. But true to his Quaker roots, he combined republicanism with egalitarianism: he wanted constitutional government, but with progressive taxes and welfare programmes; he advocated private ownership, but moderated by the common good.

Society, he insisted, was not the same as government. The desire to cooperate caused us to develop informal associations that promote social harmony. Governments are not needed for this, and indeed they violate our natural rights when they interfere. But other rights (such as property rights) still rely on government to defend them. As for the best form of government, Paine argued that republics were generally more peaceable than monarchies, and for America he proposed a representative and constitutional republic. But the power of any government should be limited to securing our civil rights. Beyond that, we could rely on the common sense of the people.

[36] Cesare Beccaria (1738–1794): Italian penal reformer and philosopher. **Key ideas:** Punishment theory; penal reform; legal reform. **Key work:** *On Crimes and Punishments* (1764).

Beccaria had a Jesuit schooling in Milan, but became interested in economics after reading **Montesquieu**. In later life, he promoted economic reform as a member of the economic council of Milan. However, today he is best remembered for his short book *On Crimes and Punishments* (1764), which was praised by **Jeremy Bentham** and had a profound effect on legal and penal systems across Europe.

Beccaria argued that the proper purpose of law and punishment is to preserve the social contract. Crime occurs when people pursue their own self-interest, but education can show them that their true interest lies in respecting the social contract. Punishment exists to serve the public good by deterring people from breaching the social contract, not to inflict harm or 'eye for an eye' retribution on those who do.

He therefore condemned torture, secret accusations, arbitrary and severe punishments, and the death penalty. Punishments should be proportionate to the crime, he insisted. For maximum deterrent effects, punishment should be swift but not necessarily severe. Crime could be cut by simplifying laws, which would make the justice system more effective, improve education and reward virtue.

[37] Thomas Jefferson (1743–1826): polymath, constitutionalist and President of the United States. **Key ideas:** Intellectual foundations of the American revolution; natural and inalienable rights; contractual basis of government; right to throw off tyrannical government; separation of powers; free press; religious tolerance. **Key works:** *Declaration of Independence* (co-author) (1776); *Notes on the State of Virginia* (1785).

Jefferson read widely on many subjects, including the arts, science and political philosophy, amassing America's largest personal library. Among his many claims to fame, he is best remembered for drafting the American Declaration of Independence, into which he inserted ideas from **John Locke** and **Algernon Sidney**. His preamble pithily encapsulated Locke's view, declaring that 'all men are created equal, that they are endowed by their Creator with certain unalienable rights, [and] that among these are life, liberty and the pursuit of happiness'. Legitimate government rested on a contract with the people: if broken, 'it is their right, it is their duty, to throw off such government, and to provide new guards for their future security'.

Jefferson distrusted both public and private power, and went on to help create a Constitution in which (following **Montesquieu**) powers were separated. He also supported public education and a free press as ways to restrain the power of government. He opposed religious intolerance, on the grounds that a person's religious views did no harm to others. He believed that people should be free to act as they pleased, provided that they did not infringe the similar freedom of others (an idea which **John Stuart Mill** later called the *no harm principle*).

Remarkably, Jefferson and his colleague John Adams (1735–1826) died within a few hours of each other on 4 July 1826, the 50th anniversary of the Declaration of Independence that they had both helped to write.

[38] Nicolas de Condorcet [Marie Jean Antoine Nicolas de Caritat, Marquis de Condorcet] (1743–1794): French mathematician, scientist and political theorist.
Key ideas: Public choice problems; female suffrage; racial equality. **Key works:** *Reflections on Negro Slavery* (1781); *Essay on the Application of Analysis to the Probability of Majority Decisions* (1785).

Condorcet is best known for his mathematical studies of election outcomes. He gave his name to the *Condorcet Paradox*, the 'rock, paper, scissors' problem that while people might prefer A to B (scissors, paper) and B to C (paper, rock), they might still prefer C to A (rock, scissors): so elections may produce no stable outcome. Condorcet devised the *Condorcet Method* of having different rounds of voting to choose the most favoured overall candidate. For these contributions, he is regarded as a pioneer of the Public Choice School, exemplified in modern times by **James Buchanan**, **Gordon Tullock** and others.

Condorcet was influenced by Physiocrat ideas and supported a liberal economy: **Turgot** appointed him Inspector General of the Paris Mint. He supported constitutional government, free public education and female suffrage. An abolitionist, he sought equal rights for all races. After the French Revolution he hoped for an enlightened rationalist government and proposed education and other reforms. However, he became caught up in the factional disputes that marred the Revolution, was arrested, and died in prison.

[39] Jeremy Bentham (1748–1832): English philosopher and social reformer. **Key idea:** Utilitarianism. **Key work:** *The Principles of Morals and Legislation* (1789).

Bentham is best known for his ethical philosophy of *utilitarianism* – that the moral standard of action was not *rights* but the amount of happiness or unhappiness that was created. Right and wrong could therefore be objectively measured: they were not something that the state could prescribe.

Bentham advocated many liberal principles, including equality between the sexes. He wrote an appeal to liberalise the laws against homosexuality (the first systematic argument on this subject), arguing that they were a disproportionate public response to private actions. He fought corruption, cruelty to animals and excessively harsh treatment of criminals. He helped found University College London as a way of opening up education to those who were neither wealthy nor members of the established

Church. He taught and inspired **John Stuart Mill**, one of the most prominent classical liberal theorists.

However, Bentham wanted to 'codify' the common law in statutes, and wrote attacks on the US Declaration of Independence and the French Declaration of Rights. Rights, he argued, were not 'natural' but were specified by lawgivers, who should assign them on the basis of 'the general mass of felicity' (i.e. their utility). To him, *natural rights* were 'simple nonsense: natural and imprescriptible rights, rhetorical nonsense – nonsense upon stilts'.

[40] James Madison (1751–1836): American constitutionalist and President of the United States. **Key ideas:** Rights as property; low and flat taxes; criticism of arbitrary power; constitutional checks and balances. **Key work:** *The Federalist* (1787–88).

Madison was a principal drafter of the Constitution of the United States, helping ensure that it embraced the separation of powers, as proposed by **Montesquieu**. He argued this case in *The Federalist*. But while 'every word' of a constitution was there to decide conflicts between power and liberty, he maintained that the only real strength of constitutions was 'the vigilance with which they are guarded by every citizen in private life'.

Madison took an innovative view on rights, describing them as a form of property: 'As a man is said to have a right to his property, he may equally be said to have a property in his rights'. Government, to him, was instituted to 'protect property of every sort' and this is the basis of liberty, since property included the individual's rights to life, liberty and freedom of speech, religion and conscience. Just as we could legitimately exclude others from trespassing on our land, so could we legitimately stop them trespassing on our rights.

Madison therefore called for a government that would 'equally respect the rights of property, and the property in rights'. So taxation, being itself an impost on property, should be very limited. Progressive taxation and redistribution would be unjust – and ineffective too, because it would reduce work incentives.

Government impositions on people's opinions, religion, person, labour and leisure should also be limited. The military draft amounted to 'arbitrary seizures of one class of citizens for the service of the rest', violating the property we have in our freedom. Equally unjust were arbitrary regulations, privileges and monopolies, which denied people an open choice of occupations and free use of what they produced.

[41] John Taylor of Caroline (1753–1824): American politician and writer. **Key ideas:** Natural rights; self-government under a limited state. **Key work:** *An Inquiry into the Principles and Policy of the Government of the United States* (1814).

Born in Virginia, Taylor studied law, but gave it up for agriculture and politics. He pioneered new farming methods, served in both the state government and the US Senate, and became the leading proponent of the 'republican' approach of his friend **Thomas Jefferson**, which advocated strict limits on central authority. He outlined an American ideal of independent, self-governing property owners living in a limited, decentralised state. His thinking merges liberal ideas of individual rights, republican ideas of good government, a conservative attachment to community and a populist suspicion of power and finance.

Taylor saw people as a mixture of good and evil, but held that a constitutional government based on virtuous principles could reduce the ill effects of self-interest and ignorance. Though he worried that the US constitution gave the president too much power, he saw it as broadly beneficial because it made the people sovereign in a republican, representative system in which power was balanced.

Taylor argued that natural rights, of which liberty was the most important, had the status of an objective moral law. Rights existed prior to government, which therefore could not deny them, but should uphold them as shields against coercion, despotism and ignorance. He denied that divisions of class or wealth were inevitable, seeing them as rooted in the privilege and corruption that came from the abuse of power.

Political and economic freedoms were inseparable, Taylor insisted. He saw paper money as a tax that redistributed wealth from farmers and workers to bankers and manufacturing capitalists. He attacked high taxes and protectionism. And he also attacked Alexander Hamilton's proposed national bank, seeing it as an unchecked agency that would indulge the privilege of the wealthy.

[42] Antoine Destutt de Tracy (1754–1836): French
Enlightenment philosopher. **Key ideas:** Property rights;
subjective value; gains from trade; anti-interventionism;
ill effects of subsidy and state monopoly. **Key works:**
Commentary on Montesquieu's 'Spirit of the Laws' (1808);
Essay on Genius, and the Works of Montesquieu (1808);
Elements of Ideology (1817–18).

De Tracy was an aristocrat who renounced his title and
entered politics. He narrowly escaped execution in the
Terror that followed the French Revolution; but during his
long imprisonment, he read **John Locke** and other liberals,
who influenced his own thinking. Economics, politics and
social issues, he thought, were unified by ideology; and
alongside **Jean-Baptiste Say**, **Condorcet**, **Madame de
Stael** and others, he formed the philosophical group called
the *Ideologues*. He popularised the ideas of **Adam Smith**
and supported republican government and free markets.
His influence was worldwide: **Thomas Jefferson** praised
his writings and had them translated.

Society, explained de Tracy, is a continual series of
exchanges. Both sides gain from this: the value of what
each gives up is less, to them, than that of what they gain:
'When I give my labor for wages it is because I esteem the
wages more than what I should have been able to produce by laboring for myself; and he who pays me prizes
more the services I render him than what he gives me in
return'. It is this that makes the exchange economy so
highly beneficial. And it is made even more productive
by entrepreneurs, who accumulate and invest capital,

employ people, and create value, which they re-invest again.

De Tracy also wrote on the evils of inflation, which he saw as a deception by the authorities, made possible by paper money. Inflation enriches debtors and taxes savers, he complained, and causes uncertainty that dampens economic activity. For the same reasons, government should have no power to control interest rates.

He described state-supported and state-privileged companies as vicious, arguing that government-created monopolies violate our natural right to buy and sell as we please. Taxes, especially on necessities, were damaging. Public works would crowd out other worthwhile projects. In a laissez-faire economy, by contrast, we would pursue the things most important to us, not be made to serve the interests of the powerful.

[43] William Godwin (1756–1836): English moral and political philosopher. **Key ideas:** Anarchism; utilitarianism; moral equality. **Key work:** *An Enquiry Concerning Political Justice* (1793).

Godwin, who began life as a nonconformist minister, was an early exponent of utilitarianism and the first modern proponent of *anarchism*. (Not the proclivity to riot and throw bombs, as many people today imagine it, but the belief that a society can flourish without any government authority.) He also wrote histories and published children's books.

Godwin's scandalous life and ideas made him infamous. He married equal rights advocate **Mary Wollstonecraft** and became friends with the romantic poets Samuel Taylor Coleridge (1772–1834), Lord Byron (1788–1824), Robert Southey (1774–1843) and Percy Bysshe Shelley (1792–1822), who paid off his debts and eloped with his daughter Mary (1797–1851), the future author of *Frankenstein*. When Godwin's wife died, he wrote a shocking biography recounting her various affairs and suicide bids, which led to him being shunned by polite society.

In *An Enquiry Concerning Political Justice* (1793), Godwin attacked all political institutions. He thought it intolerable that some individuals should control others. Birth and rank, he insisted, should not affect how people are treated. Monarchy was corrupt and aristocratic privilege unjust. Indeed, any form of government, he argued, corrupts society by perpetuating dependence and ignorance.

Accordingly, Godwin urged the complete overthrow of law, property and other institutions. This *anarchy* – meaning the absence of authority – would work by discussion, not compulsion. It would require free speech and candid talk, but people were capable of recognising truth, and technological progress gave them more time to spend on finding it. Moral understanding would replace the need for politics. Actions would be decided on rational utilitarian principles: 'If justice has any meaning', he wrote, 'it is just that I should contribute everything in my power to the benefit of the whole'.

[44] Mary Wollstonecraft (1759–1797): English advocate of female rights. **Key ideas:** Feminism; equal rights; republicanism. **Key works:** *A Vindication of the Rights of Men* (1790); *A Vindication of the Rights of Women* (1792).

Mary Wollstonecraft, the wife of **William Godwin** (and mother of their daughter Mary Shelley) was a radical thinker who led an unconventional life. She was a novelist and an early feminist political philosopher, who believed that the rights of men should extend equally to women. Her views were inspired by the sermons of **Richard Price**, who introduced her to Joseph Johnson, a radical publisher, enabling her to develop and spread her ideas more widely.

In *A Vindication of the Rights of Men* (1790), Wollstonecraft proposed replacing the aristocratic system with a republic, and attacked the traditionalism of Edmund Burke as stifling progress and rationality. In *A Vindication of the Rights of Women* (1792), she stressed how essential women were in society and for the education of children; and that as rational human beings, they deserved the same rights as men. She advocated greater female education, not for the benefit of men, but of women – insisting that it should be 'education after the same model' as men's. Women, she thought, were being held back by society's focus on beauty and modesty and other false, middle-class values. 'The civilised women of the present century', she wrote, 'with few exceptions, are only anxious to inspire love, when they ought to cherish a nobler ambition, and by their abilities and virtues exact respect'.

[45] Germaine de Staël (1766–1817): Swiss–French intellectual and novelist. **Key ideas:** Republican liberalism; representative government; private property as foundation for rights; constitutional monarchy; anti-absolutism; decentralisation. **Key work:** *Considerations on the Principal Events of the French Revolution* (1817).

Unusually for a woman at the time, de Staël became one of the leading intellectuals and writers of her age. Her influence was international and at the highest levels: she sparred with Napoleon Bonaparte (1769–1821), corresponded with **Thomas Jefferson**, and knew the Russian Tsar Alexander I (1777–1825). Her sparkling personality and intellect, and fame as a novelist and political thinker, made her a catch for the salons of Germany, England, Sweden, Russia and Austria. She formed romantic attachments with some of the leading figures of the day, including Johann Goethe (1749–1832), William Pitt (1759–1806) and **Benjamin Constant**. As a contemporary put it, 'There are three great powers in Europe: England, Russia, and Madame de Staël'.

She was born into a wealthy family. Her father, the Swiss banker Jacques Necker (1732–1804), was finance minister to Louis XVI (1754–1793) and the author of books on liberty, government and the constitution. After Necker was dismissed from the royal service, the family removed themselves to Switzerland. Her parents pushed her to marry a Swedish diplomat who – though twice her age – raised her social status. She began writing on the political crisis, but Napoleon's agents monitored her activities, prompting her to continue her exile.

In 1814 she returned to Paris under the Bourbon restoration and in 1817 completed *Considerations on the Principal Events of the French Revolution*. The book became the foundation of modern French liberalism. It argued that the Revolution was the inevitable result of the same social, cultural and political factors that had produced the bloodless revolution in England a century before. De Staël saw the many abuses of power by French monarchs, such as arbitrary imprisonment and banishment, as a partial justification of the Revolution; but she was equally critical of the absolute power grabbed by Bonaparte after the political turmoil.

France was ruled by arbitrary power, she explained, not by law. The only system that could resolve the lasting political tensions was the liberal system of constitutionalism, political moderation, representative government, the rule of law and private property. Economic prosperity, she argued, was based on the rule of law, morality and political freedom, shored up by free speech and a free press, which bound the political representatives to the will of the governed. This in turn encouraged social harmony: 'Nothing but liberty', she wrote, 'can arouse the soul to the interests of social order'.

[46] Wilhelm von Humboldt (1767–1835): Prussian philosopher, educationalist, diplomat and linguist. **Key ideas:** Freedom essential to moral development; the night-watchman state. **Key work:** *On the Limits of State Action* (1850).

Humboldt was much influenced by **John Locke**. His posthumous book, *On the Limits of State Action* (1850), influenced **John Stuart Mill**, whose essay *On Liberty* (1859) spread Humboldt's ideas to English speakers.

The state, he wrote, should be limited to providing security to the individuals who comprise it. The highest purpose of human beings was self-cultivation and moral development. Freedom was essential to this purpose, as was having a wide range of experiences and options to learn from. So we must tolerate diversity. 'Freedom is the grand and indispensable condition', he wrote. But freedom meant diversity: 'Even the most free and self-reliant of men is thwarted and hindered in his development by uniformity of position'.

Liberty, to Humboldt, was the condition in which people enjoyed 'the most absolute freedom' to develop their individuality as they chose, restricted only by their rights and abilities, and without anyone else preventing them from doing so. The state should therefore have only a *night-watchman* role, protecting us against trespass, but not interfering in our self-development.

[47] Benjamin Constant [Henri Benjamin Constant de Rebecque] (1767–1830): Swiss–French novelist, politician, political writer and activist. **Key ideas:** Constitutions to restrain government; checks and balances; right to resist illegitimate government. **Key work:** *The Principles of Politics Applicable to All Governments* (1815).

Constant was one of the first thinkers to call himself a 'liberal'. Well-travelled, he studied in Germany and Scotland, where he discovered the ideas of **Adam Ferguson** and **Adam Smith**. Though a believer in constitutional monarchy and an aristocratic upper house of the legislature, he made important contributions to liberal political theory.

In particular, Constant argued that constitutions do not exist to *empower* our leaders, but to *restrain* them. Even popular government would turn into majority despotism unless restrained: as **Montesquieu** had argued, power needs constitutional checks and balances to contain it. None of us, Constant insisted, had any entitlement to rule over any other: it had to be a matter of consent. If government lost the consent of the public, it lost its entire authority, and its coercive power became illegitimate. People had a right to resist governments that abuse their freedoms – another valuable restraint on government power.

But even all that took us only so far. People's busy lives, he warned, left them little time for active participation in politics. So *freedom* was more valuable to them than having a political *voice*. Constant drew up a long list of the basic freedoms: personal freedom, religious freedom, free speech and opinion, property rights, and immunity from arbitrary decisions by those in authority.

[48] Jean-Baptiste Say (1767–1832): French businessman and economist. **Key ideas:** Say's Law; supply side economics; liberal incentives to progress. **Key work:** *A Treatise on Political Economy* (1803).

Best known for the Law named after him (encapsulated by one twentieth-century economist as 'supply creates its own demand'), Say was born into a Protestant family in Lyon. Destined for a life in commerce, he worked for sugar merchants in England, then insurers in France. But his career changed when he was appointed secretary to the French finance minister, followed by other government jobs – until his writings (expounding the liberal principles of **Adam Smith**) annoyed Napoleon Bonaparte (1769–1821), whereupon he returned to business, running a large cotton mill.

Say's Law suggests that production is the source of all demand (something that earlier writers such as **James Mill** and **John Stuart Mill** had already hinted at). As Say explains, individuals earn money only when they create a successful good or service – and only then can they afford to buy other goods and services.

There are two important liberal conclusions from this. First, productivity and investment are the only ways to boost prosperity, while government spending and regulation may actually damage it. Second, the economy is self-regulating: if there is over-production in one market, it will return to balance without government intervention – either because producers will supply less or because customers will not be able to afford so much.

Say also advocated monetary restraint, since inflation distorts relative price signals (a point taken up later by **Ludwig von Mises** and **F. A. Hayek**). He advocated monetary stability, private property, unregulated prices, competition, low taxes and balanced budgets so that entrepreneurs were incentivised to innovate and invest in better solutions to people's needs.

[49] David Ricardo (1772–1823): English economist, stockbroker and politician. **Key ideas:** Economic theory; free trade; comparative advantage. **Key work:** *On the Principles of Political Economy and Taxation* (1817).

Ricardo's career began as a successful broker and speculator. It was said that he made £1 million by misleading market players into thinking that the French had won the Battle of Waterloo, and then buying stocks and bonds cheaply.

His career as an economist started when he read **Adam Smith**'s *Wealth of Nations* (1776). Applying rigorous logic to Smith's ideas, he made important developments in the theory of rents, wages, profits, taxation and value. In 1809 he argued that the high inflation in England was the result of the over-issuance of banknotes – making him an early monetarist. Like Smith, he opposed protectionism, arguing that the Corn Laws (which restricted wheat imports) made domestic production inefficient and drove up rents.

Ricardo's greatest contribution to liberal thinking was perhaps his theory of comparative costs (now known as *comparative advantage*). Countries, he said, could make themselves better off by specialising in what they can produce *relatively* cheaper (in terms of what else they might have produced) than other countries. Even if a country can produce everything more cheaply (in *absolute* terms) than another, it is still better to specialise and trade in the goods where they have a comparative advantage. This principle became and remains one of the key foundations of the argument for free trade.

[50] James Mill (1773–1836): Scottish economist, historian, political scientist and philosopher. **Key ideas:** law and prison reform; utilitarianism; toleration and free speech; representative government; parliamentary reform. **Key works:** *Elements of Political Economy* (1821*); Essay on Government, Jurisprudence, Liberty of the Press, Education, and Prisons and Prison Discipline* (1823).

James Mill's mother, determined to advance the prospects of this shoemaker's son, gave him a rigorous education and even changed the family name from Milne to Mill to make it sound less parochially Scottish. James became a noted Greek scholar at the University of Edinburgh, and a licenced preacher; but his real talent lay in teaching and writing.

Moving to London, he authored a pamphlet criticising export subsidies, and became a regular contributor to reviews and journals. In a simple, clear and logical style, he wrote entries for the *Encyclopaedia Britannica* on politics, law and education, and papers on prison reform (arguing that criminality was due to poor education, and that prisons should re-educate criminals, not harm them). He wrote a massive three-volume book on *The History of British India* (1818) and, despite his criticisms of British rule, joined the Indian civil service in London.

In his early 30s he met **Jeremy Bentham**, who shared his beliefs in religious toleration, law reform, free speech, a free press and democratic reform. He became Bentham's closest friend and the leading advocate of his utilitarianism, turning Bentham's brusque ideas into a widely popular philosophy.

Mill's *Essay on Government* (1820) was a wide survey of politics. Using utilitarian principles, he argued that government existed to promote the happiness of individuals in the community. Since people naturally wanted to obtain happiness with minimal effort, and would gladly live off the labour of others (whose happiness is thereby diminished), government should aim at maximising happiness by limiting such exploitation. Monarchy and aristocracy could not achieve this because they were built on exploitation; but direct democracy absorbed too much of people's time and effort. A representative government was therefore best.

However, individuals were the best judges of their own interests, and representatives needed to be restrained from imposing their own interests on others. So Mill argued for radical reform, including frequent elections, short terms and a wider franchise – though to the dismay of his son **John Stuart Mill** he did not include votes for women. Mill's ideas critically advanced the case for radical parliamentary reform that led to the 1832 Reform Bill.

7 THE AGE OF REFORM

In America, the first half of the nineteenth century saw a marked growth in anti-slavery movements and ideas. Many abolitionists also supported equal rights and political participation for women, seeing gender as providing no more justification for unequal treatment than race. Many appealed to religious principles, others to natural law or the liberal principles on which the US was founded. Some abolitionists, however, saw women's rights as a radical and controversial issue that could poison the anti-slavery cause. In the event, slavery was abolished in the US in 1865, but women had to wait until 1920 until their right to vote was written into the Constitution.

In Britain, a landmark court judgment of 1772 ruled that slavery had no legal standing there. By 1808, Parliament had outlawed the international slave trade, and there was a growing movement to outlaw slavery in British possessions too, which succeeded with the Slavery Abolition Act of 1833.

Liberal *economic* ideas were also challenging the old order. In post-revolutionary France, greater social mobility made some thinkers such as **Frédéric Bastiat** ask why monopolies and protectionism should continue. In rapidly industrialising Britain, **Richard Cobden** and **John Bright** argued likewise that agricultural protections no longer served the public interest, but undermined it. The new railways enabled such reformist campaigns to go national. With all the profound changes in society that had been brought by the Industrial Revolution, it was time for a national and international debate on the role of the state.

[51] William Ellery Channing (1780–1842): American Unitarian preacher, theologian, abolitionist and social reformer. **Key ideas:** Gender equality; right to life; abolition of slavery. **Key work:** *Slavery* (1835).

Channing was one of the pioneers of the women's movement, making the first public case for gender equality. He based this largely on religious principles, saying that the universality of the soul showed that men and women were equal in the eyes of God, but that 'instinct, interest and force' had prevented this being reflected in society.

Channing also took up the anti-slavery cause with books and sermons. By the nature of property rights, he argued, human beings could not be the property of other human beings. Though he still believed that Africans could not survive emancipation without supervision, Britain's peaceful abolition of slavery in the Caribbean convinced him to call for immediate emancipation in the US too.

[52] Sarah Grimké (1792–1873): American abolitionist and leader of the women's suffrage movement and
[53] Angelina Grimké (1805–1879): American abolitionist

and suffragist. **Key ideas:** Abolitionism and women's rights. **Key works:** *The Equality of the Sexes and the Condition of Women* (Sarah, 1839); *An Appeal to the Christian Women of the South* (Angelina, 1836).

Sarah Grimké was a prominent American abolitionist who came to lead the women's suffrage movement. Born into a slave-owning household in South Carolina, she (illicitly) helped to teach slaves to read. Moving north to Philadelphia, she became a Quaker. But she and her sister Angelina came into conflict with the Quaker leadership for writing letters to the newspapers and the clergy on the condition of women. Sarah's 1839 book, *The Equality of the Sexes and the Condition of Women*, circulated widely. She argued that female emancipation was no different from the anti-slavery cause: women too were reasoning moral agents, with rights and responsibilities. Some abolitionists, however, saw the Grimké sisters' radical feminism as an unhelpful distraction.

Angelina was also a prominent abolitionist and women's rights campaigner. Following **Hugo Grotius**, she argued that 'every slaveholder is a man-stealer' because 'a man is a man, and as a man he has inalienable rights, among which is the right to personal liberty'. Slave owners robbed two million people of that right. The person who first captures a slave, she said, commits an act of robbery; but the slave owner 'perpetrates the same crime continually'.

[54] Frédéric Bastiat (1801–1850): French political economist and free trader. **Key ideas:** Against protectionism; free trade and investment; opportunity cost. **Key works:**

Economic Sophisms (1845); *The State* (1848); *The Law* (1850).

Orphaned on both sides by the age of ten, Bastiat was brought up by relatives, and worked in his uncle's export business, where he learnt about the impact of tax and regulation on commerce. His uncle died when Frédéric was 24 and left him family estates, which enabled him to indulge his intellectual pursuits in philosophy, history, politics and political economy. He became politically active as a Justice of the Peace and later a Liberal member of the National Assembly after the 1848 Revolution.

Yet it is as a brilliant economic and political commentator and pamphleteer that he is most remembered. His writings were mostly popular essays and satires, some collected in *Economic Sophisms* (1845), in which he demolished regulation and protectionism, and demonstrated the benefits of free markets. His essays became best sellers thanks to their acerbic wit and penetrating argument – often based on exaggeration and *reductio ad absurdum*, in which protectionist policies are taken to their logical but plainly ridiculous conclusion.

A famous example was *The Petition of the Candle-Makers* (1846), a parody in which a trade association of candle-makers and tallow producers petition the Chamber of Deputies to protect them against unfair competition. But the competitor they complain of is *the sun*. They argue that regulation is needed to make people draw their blinds through the day so that they use more candles, boosting their industry and the employment it generates. In another parable, he warned that the construction of a railway between France and Spain would encourage the movement of goods between them – but that producers on both sides would then surely demand tariffs to save their industries from cheap imports, leaving consumers no better off.

His famous article *That Which Is Seen and That Which Is Not Seen* (1850) contains the 'parable of the broken window' – an early statement of the *opportunity cost* idea developed by the Austrian economist Friedrich von Wieser (1851–1926) in 1914 and now a standard principle in economics. If a careless boy breaks a shop window, says Bastiat, it creates six francs' worth of work for the glazier – who now has six francs more to spend in the local economy, boosting other local businesses too. But what is *seen* does not mean that we should deliberately promote window breaking as a way of creating economic growth (though this same principle 'unhappily, regulates the greater part of our economical institutions'). For what is *not seen* is the fact that the shopkeeper now has six francs *less* to spend in the local economy, completely negating the gain.

What *would* boost economic growth, thought Bastiat, were free markets and free trade. He became a leader of France's Free Trade Association and corresponded with **Richard Cobden**. He argued that free trade and commerce would generate revenues that could be invested both in capital and labour – further boosting economic efficiency and benefiting the working population.

In *The State* (1848), Bastiat criticised the state as 'the great fiction by which everyone seeks to live at the expense of everyone else', and in *The Law* (1850) he outlined a legal system that he thought would regulate a free society. Individuals, he argued, had the right to protect their own persons, liberty and property – rights that exist prior to laws and governments. The purpose of the state was only to provide a 'common force' to protect these rights.

The state had no right to take money and property from some people for the benefit of others – that would be 'legal plunder'. And a government that tried to do more than merely protect our rights – spending on what it thinks are philanthropic works, for example – had no logical stopping point. Given the inertness of the electorate, the power of law, and the supposed infallibility of democratic lawmakers, the end result would be statism, with the public moulded to the will of their rulers 'like the clay to the potter'.

Bastiat died of tuberculosis aged 49, at the most intellectually productive time of his life.

[55] Harriet Martineau (1802–1876): English social theorist and political economist. **Key ideas:** Liberal feminism; fictional illustrations of liberal economists. **Key work:** *Illustrations of Political Economy* (1832–34).

Harriet Martineau is remembered for her large output of books and essays on liberal political, economic and sociological themes. Her feminine point of view was rare among contemporary writers, and her works did much to change attitudes towards women and the education of girls. She translated (and arguably improved) the work of the sociologist Auguste Comte (1798–1857), and is often considered the first female sociologist.

The failure of her father's textile business prompted her to become a full-time writer. Unusually for a woman at the time, she was able to support herself through her writing – her books becoming many times more popular than those of the novelist and campaigner Charles Dickens (1812–1870).

Martineau's *Illustrations of Political Economy* series began in 1832 with a fictional treatment of the ideas of Adam Smith. It soon achieved success and acclaim, and helped popularise Smith internationally. She followed this with other fictional illustrations of James Mill, Jeremy Bentham and David Ricardo. These works brought women of the time into the world of economics by showing how the domestic economy reflects wider economic themes.

On a lengthy visit to the US, Martineau met **James Madison**, and many of the leading New England abolitionists. She studied and wrote about the education of girls, complaining how the norms of the time left girls undereducated, passive and subservient to men.

As a sociologist, she studied families, religion and race. She held that society was shaped by general social laws, and that to understand it one must take account of broad themes such as science, population, and the religious and social institutions, including the role of women.

[56] Richard Cobden (1804–1865): English manufacturer and politician and **[57] John Bright** (1811–1889): English reformer and politician. **Key ideas:** Wealth-creating benefits of free trade; the case against protectionism; Manchester Liberalism; repeal of the Corn Laws. **Key works:** *England, Ireland and America, by a Manchester*

Manufacturer (Cobden, 1835); *Speeches on Parliamentary Reform* (Bright, 1866).

Richard Cobden grew wealthy through his share in a calico printing business in Manchester, the world centre of textile production. His international travels, and his reading of **Adam Smith**, convinced him of the merits of free trade.

In 1838, Cobden founded the Anti-Corn Law League together with John Bright, who had become the leading orator of the Free Trade Movement. The Corn Laws were high tariffs on imported wheat: introduced ostensibly to protect British agriculture, they pushed up the price of bread, but were defended by powerful landowners, whose rents they inflated. The League became a major campaigning force for reform, producing pamphlets and holding rallies across the country.

Cobden argued that ending agricultural protection would not only alleviate poverty in rural areas; it would make agriculture more efficient and would increase the demand for manufactures, both from farmers and from a better-off rural population in general. It would also boost trade with other countries, and thereby help to create peace and understanding between nations.

Cobden and Bright's approach became known as *Manchester Liberalism*, or the *Manchester School*. In the 1840s, the two entered Parliament, where Bright became a formidable reformist orator, backed up by Cobden's arguments. In 1846, after a bad harvest and blight in the potato crop, their efforts succeeded and the Corn Laws were repealed.

Cobden later helped to open up commerce between Britain and France, and preached his free-trade ideas in France, Spain, Italy and Russia. Bright became instrumental in constitutional reforms to give greater inclusion to the working class, and in ending the political discrimination against Irish Catholics.

[58] Alexis de Tocqueville (1805–1859): French political thinker. **Key ideas:** Constitutional reforms, bicameral government; need for limits on majoritarian democracy. **Key work:** *Democracy in America* (1835 and 1840).

De Tocqueville is best known for his two-volume *Democracy in America* (1835 and 1840), based on his observations while travelling in the US. An early work of sociology and political science, it explored the strengths and weaknesses of American politics, in particular the tension between freedom and equality, and drew lessons for the democratic restructuring of post-revolutionary France.

De Tocqueville was born into an aristocratic Normandy family, who fled to England during the French Revolution, but later returned to France. Though his parents remained royalists, Alexis became an active critic of the constitutional monarchy that ruled France from 1814. After the 1848 Revolution, he served briefly in the new government, and worked on a new constitution.

His aristocratic background but liberal views are reflected in the tension he saw between elitism and populism, and between freedom and equality. While he advocated liberal, parliamentary government, he thought that democracy must be restrained – popularising the phrase 'the tyranny of the majority' coined by John Adams (1735–1826). To reduce that threat, he called for a bicameral parliament and a president elected by popular vote. More generally, he called for diversity in political systems and the decentralisation of power.

His work on American democracy began when he secured a commission to examine the prison system in the US – though this was mainly a pretext to study American society and politics. In the same spirit of enquiry he also made visits to England, Algeria and Ireland.

De Tocqueville sought to learn not just about the potential threats *to* democracy, but the threats *of* it. While he admired the self-confidence that democratic equality had brought Americans, he worried that the decline of the old social hierarchies left democracy unconstrained. The only authority, moral or political, in a society where everyone's opinion (however ill-informed) counts the same, would be the majority. But individuals would be unable to stand up to the majority, or defend their rights against it.

This swamping of individuals by the crowd was made more likely, thought Tocqueville, because democratic equality encouraged the materialism of the expanding middle class and an 'individualism' (i.e. self-absorption) in which people thought more about themselves and less about the wider health of society. Democracy would therefore slide into unthinking populism. This majoritarian despotism would smother invention and self-expression.

De Tocqueville felt that America also suffered from an excessive drive for equality but an insufficient commitment to freedom. It needed a new kind of political science that would inject *social values* into democracy. People should be free to pursue their own self-interest, but it should be 'self interest rightly understood' – one moderated by social values, foresight and self-command.

Another restraint on runaway populism was *civil society*, which de Tocqueville found strong in America. He was struck by how Americans were constantly forming associations 'to give entertainments, to found seminaries, to build inns, to construct churches, to diffuse books, to send missionaries to the antipodes; in this manner they found hospitals, prisons, and schools'.

He thought that America's constitutional framework, with its independent judiciary, decentralised decision-making, bicameral government and popularly elected president, was a good basis for a democratic constitution in France. But (perhaps reflecting his aristocratic roots), he felt that too much power was vested in the legislature, where the short electoral cycle produced mediocre legislators. France should aim for a stronger executive, he thought; but just as important were freedom of association, of religion and of the press.

[59] William Lloyd Garrison (1805–1879): American abolitionist and journalist. **Key ideas:** Abolition; women's rights; passive resistance. **Key work:** *The Liberator* (1831–65).

William Lloyd Garrison was only an infant when his father, a merchant seaman, abandoned his family, leaving

William's devout Baptist mother struggling to care for them. At age 13, after some unsuccessful ventures, he was apprenticed to the editor of the *Newburyport Herald*, where he learnt how to run a newspaper. In his 20s he borrowed to acquire his own paper, which he called the *Newburyport Free Press*, though it failed because of editorial arguments with backers.

Garrison moved to Boston as a printer and editor for a pro-temperance and pro-reform paper, and met *Genius of Emancipation* author Benjamin Lundy (1789–1839), who brought him into the abolitionist cause. Garrison helped found the New England Antislavery Society and started *The Liberator*, which would become the leading abolitionist newspaper.

Garrison argued that slavery violated the right of all individuals to be free. He initially advocated relocating American slaves in West Africa, but abandoned this idea because some proponents saw it as a way of removing free black people.

His call for women to petition against slavery sparked a debate over women's political rights. *The Liberator* published the articles of the **Grimké sisters** and became the leading advocate of emancipation. This, and Garrison's anti-constitutionalism – he argued, along with **Frederick Douglass**, that the US Constitution inherently supported slavery and that the Union should be dissolved – split the abolitionist movement, some of whom feared that these causes were confusing the abolitionist message. The schisms were further deepened by Garrison's rejection of direct action and violence.

Though a pacifist, Garrison was radical and outspoken: 'I am aware that many object to the severity of my language; but is there not cause for severity? I will be as harsh as truth, and as uncompromising as justice ... And I *will* be heard'. Indeed, he was so outspoken that the slave state of Georgia put a price on his head. In 1835 a mob of thousands surrounded a Boston building where he was speaking and dragged him through the streets by a rope, before the authorities intervened.

After slavery was abolished, the anti-slavery movement was again split when Garrison argued that its purpose was now over. He withdrew, but remained involved in other reform movements such as civil rights and female suffrage. In Europe, he met **John Bright**, **John Stuart Mill**, **Herbert Spencer** and other liberals. He argued, against Karl Marx (1818–1883), that commerce brings mutual benefit to all classes, and advocated abolishing all restrictions on free trade.

[60] John Stuart Mill (1806–1873): English philosopher and reformer. **Key ideas:** Choice and responsibility; tyranny of the majority; the no-harm principle; problems of paternalism; free speech; free association; lifestyle freedom; representative government; federalism; utilitarianism. **Key works:** *On Liberty* (1859); *Considerations on Representative Government* (1861); *Utilitarianism* (1863).

John Stuart Mill was taught at home by his father **James Mill**, assisted by **Jeremy Bentham**. His education was intense: at the age of three he was taught Greek; at eight,

Latin; by ten he could read all the classical authors; by twelve he was studying logic and political economy; and by fourteen he was taking courses in science and mathematics. But this accelerated learning had its price: at age twenty he suffered a nervous breakdown, later blaming it on his lack of a real childhood.

Though he had been drilled in empiricism, utilitarianism and reason, and not exposed to religion or other 'irrational' ideas, in adult life he came to value human diversity, spontaneity, individuality, originality and uniqueness over rationality. Like **Wilhelm von Humboldt**, Mill stressed the importance of human beings' personal and moral development, and saw freedom as essential to this. He thought that people would never learn and develop unless they were responsible for their own actions. Human beings were defined by their ability to make choices – over their lifestyle, for example – so to properly exercise their humanity, they needed a variety of options to choose from. It was the diversity of Europe, he argued, that gave it its 'progressive and many-sided development'.

Isaiah Berlin called Mill's *On Liberty* (1859) 'the clearest, most candid, persuasive and moving exposition of the point of view of those who desire an open and tolerant society'. Mill began it by warning (like **de Tocqueville**) that, while the old threats to liberty were monarchy and aristocracy, the new threat was the tyranny of the majority. The majority not only dominated political decision-making, it shaped the culture too, turning people into 'industrious sheep' with no opinions of their own.

Mill defined *liberty* early on in the book. Individuals should be free to do as they wish, he argued, *provided they do not harm others*. Families, groups and governments were subject to the same no-harm rule:

> The sole end for which mankind are warranted, individually or collectively, in interfering with the liberty of action of any of their number, is self-protection ... [T]he only purpose for which power can be rightfully exercised over any member of a civilised community, against his will, is to prevent harm to others.

Harm, to Mill, meant physical harm, not mere offence. Physical harm is plain to see but offence is not: so the rule could be abused unless this line were drawn strictly. He also rejected paternalism – interfering with someone's freedom 'for their own good' – for several reasons: it was too easy to abuse state power on these grounds; even well-intentioned rulers might mistake what was actually good for citizens; and to be whole human beings, not mere ciphers, people must make their own choices and take responsibility for them.

The no-harm principle also applies to the *risk* of causing physical harm – such as (in Mill's famous example) by shouting 'Fire!' in a crowded theatre. It could even extend to allowing people to come to harm, if that were easy to prevent – saving a child drowning in a pond, for instance. But Mill did not specify exactly where the boundaries lay – how much risk was acceptable before we intervene, or how much effort we should make to prevent harm happening to others.

Mill believed that the no-harm principle protected our basic rights to life, person and property. He defended freedom of association, and freedom in taste, pursuits and life plans. He also passionately defended freedom of speech, arguing that open discourse was essential for our intellectual and social progress. It was dangerous to censor or prevent free speech: the censored opinion might actually be true, he argued; or it may be false but contain some part of the truth; its challenge to our received opinions would force us to ensure our opinions are robust; and opinions that remain unchallenged would become mere dogma, without moral or intellectual power.

In *Considerations on Representative Government* (1861) Mill outlined his support for limited and representative democracy. Direct democracy was impractical for a large, sophisticated community, he counselled: representative democracy allowed policy questions to be debated in detail, but still left citizens involved in the political process, which was important for developing their moral capacity. Such a democracy, he thought, should have a *federal* system so that local issues could be decided locally; but some central restraint was needed to ensure that local minorities were protected against the whims of local majorities. Even so, the key role of government was not to empower majorities: it was to create the conditions that would promote diversity and free choice.

Mill may have been drawn towards this approach by his soulmate (and, later, wife) **Harriet Taylor**. He certainly shared her feminism. In *The Subjection of Women* (1869), he explained why women should enjoy perfect equality.

Mill also developed the *utilitarianism* of his mentor, **Jeremy Bentham**. He doubted that happiness could easily be measured and calculated, since humans were diverse and their calculations fallible. There were, he thought, 'higher' and 'lower' pleasures which affected the calculus: 'Better Socrates dissatisfied than a pig satisfied'. Higher pleasures were to be preferred, because nobody who had tried both would choose the lower, he suggested. But, even so modified, Mill's utilitarianism seems at odds with his defence of *rights* (which Bentham, more consistently, had dismissed as 'nonsense'): how far can we violate individual rights in the name of social utility or the general happiness?

[61] Harriet Taylor Mill (1807–1858): English feminist and reformer. **Key ideas:** Female education and suffrage; worker co-ownership. **Key work:** *The Enfranchisement of Women* (1851).

Harriet Taylor broke the convention that women should conform and attend to domestic duties, arguing instead for their enfranchisement and independence. Male dominance in the home, she insisted, closed off women's opportunities for education and personal development, and because women were denied political power (including the vote), laws continued to be made for the benefit of men.

Raised a Unitarian, Harriet married John Taylor (1787–1849) when she was 18 and he was already 39. It was an unhappy union, and, soon after, she began a relationship (highly scandalous at the time) with **John Stuart Mill**. They married two years after John Taylor died.

The Enfranchisement of Women (1851), a radical call for political equality for women in elections, political office and law, appeared under Mill's name, though he acknowledged her as the author. He similarly revealed her authorship or co-authorship of a number of newspaper articles, and a pamphlet criticising the law on violence against women and children. A chapter of Mill's *Principles of Political Economy* (1848), advocating universal education and worker co-ownership of industry, also reflects her views. While it is difficult to assess how much influence Harriet had on her husband's writings, he lavished enormous praise on her after her death, saying that when two people have such similar views, it 'is of little consequence ... which of them holds the pen'.

[62] Lysander Spooner (1808–1887): American anarchist, abolitionist and legal theorist. **Key ideas:** Deregulation and competition; vices are not crimes; slavery and the constitution; anarchism. **Key work:** *The Unconstitutionality of Slavery* (1845).

Spooner practised law in Massachusetts – defying state laws that imposed lengthy apprenticeships on non-graduates. He complained that such laws protected rich graduates from poor competitors, and went on to argue against all licensing of lawyers, doctors and other professions, seeing it as a denial of the natural right of contract. He even founded his own mail company to take on the monopoly of the United States Post Office – though the government saw off the competition with legal challenges.

Spooner opposed all regulations that made it harder for people to start their own businesses. Usury laws, for example, meant that lenders could not charge higher interest rates to compensate themselves for the higher risk and lack of security involved in lending to a new business: the result was fewer start-ups, less competition, and only the established few being able to borrow.

Spooner denied the right of any government to intervene in the personal actions of individuals, unless they caused genuine harm to others. While *crimes* were actions motivated by the intention to harm the person or property of someone else, *vices* implied no such malice, and only the acting individual was (potentially) harmed. Since in law 'there can be no crime without a criminal intent' and 'no one ever practices a vice with such criminal intent', intervention was unjustified. Indeed, it would open the door to tyranny: 'Unless this clear distinction between vices and crimes be made and recognized by the laws, there can be on earth no such thing as individual right, liberty or property, no such things as the right of one man to the control of his own person and property...'

Moreover, the long-term consequences of intervening are often unclear, making it 'difficult, in nearly all cases, to determine where virtue ends, and vice begins'. We can only determine it in ourselves, and should leave others to decide what promotes their long-term happiness or unhappiness: 'If this great right is not to be left free and open to all', he concluded, 'then each man's whole right, as a reasoning human being, to "liberty and the pursuit of happiness", is denied him'.

Today, Spooner is best remembered for his 1845 book, *The Unconstitutionality of Slavery*. Many abolitionists believed that the Constitution of the United States legally recognised slavery, and that only an amendment or a new union of non-slave states could correct this. But Spooner argued that, whatever the Founders had said while drafting it, the actual text did not endorse slavery. It was therefore up to the *slave states* to secede and form a new union. Accordingly, he opposed the Civil War as a coercive centralist attempt to preserve the existing union by denying states their natural right to throw off a government.

Such ideas strengthened Spooner's anarchism. In 1870 he argued that the Constitution was a contract that, logically, could bind only those who signed it, and so had no contemporary force. And since the government had used coercion to maintain its power, contrary to natural law and the consent of the governed, the Constitution plainly provided no security against tyranny. He also maintained that juries should not only rule on the arguments presented in court, but also on the legitimacy of the law – and even refuse to convict someone prosecuted under a law that they considered unjust.

[63] Henry David Thoreau (1817–1862): American philosopher, abolitionist, tax resister and anarchist. **Key ideas:** Civil disobedience; anarchism; abolitionism; injustice of majority voting. **Key work:** *Civil Disobedience* (1849).

Thoreau was born in Concord, Massachusetts, where his father had a pencil-making business (in which he participated) and his mother was an anti-slavery reformer who sheltered fugitive slaves escaping to Canada. He studied at Harvard, and briefly taught in a school, before taking up an invitation to tutor the children of the essayist and speaker Ralph Waldo Emerson (1803–1882), who inspired him with radical ideas.

His first love, however, was the countryside. As described in his book *Walden* (1854), he withdrew to a self-sufficient life in the woods. He also wanted to 'withdraw and stand aloof' from a government whose values (particularly on slavery and war) he despised. But he was imprisoned for not paying his poll tax. Though soon released when a friend paid the tax for him, this episode inspired him to write *Civil Disobedience* (1849), in which he outlined a robust anarchism. 'That government is best which governs not at all', he wrote. '[T]he authority of government ... must have the sanction and consent of the governed. ... I, Henry Thoreau, do not wish to be regarded as a member of any incorporated society which I have not joined'. A legitimate government should be able to tolerate those who, like him, refused it allegiance.

Governments, he wrote, merely created obstacles to action, trade and progress. He criticised majority rule as based on might, rather than justice. A legitimate state should guarantee individuals' rights, not the majority's power. Unjust laws should be broken: even paying tax implies consent for government injustices.

[64] Frederick Douglass (1818–1895): Afro-American abolitionist and reformer. **Key ideas:** Abolitionism; human choice and responsibility. **Key works:** *Narrative* *of the Life of Frederick Douglass, An American Slave* (1845); *My Bondage and My Freedom* (1855); *Life and Times of Frederick Douglass* (1881).

Douglass was born into slavery but escaped and made his way to the Quaker city of Philadelphia, where he joined abolitionist groups and became a preacher and prominent anti-slavery speaker. In the mid 1800s he made visits to Britain and Ireland, arguing the abolitionist cause.

Though primarily a campaigner, Douglass developed the liberal argument that slavery violates the principle of human responsibility: individuals cannot be regarded as morally complete if directed by another. He also pressed for the political rights of women, arguing that governments were denying themselves half of humanity's intellectual power. He accepted the liberal principles of self-ownership, the right to use one's own labour, limited government and self-reliance. He supported private property, and indeed saw it as a human duty to make provision for the future.

Though **William Lloyd Garrison** became an early friend, Douglass thought Garrison's pacifist anarchism was inadequate, given how the state sanctioned slavery – and how, even after abolition, the laws and institutions (such as trade unions) continued to discriminate racially. He insisted that the state should actively combat the inequality it had created, calling for *restitution* in the form of land grants and a closer adherence to the US Constitution. His vision was equality and freedom: 'Give the Negro fair play', he said, 'and let him alone'.

[65] Gustave de Molinari (1819–1912): Belgian free-market economist. **Key ideas:** Anarcho-capitalism; critique of the state, power and privilege; private security. **Key works:** *The Production of Security* (1849); *The Society of Tomorrow* (1899).

According to **Murray Rothbard**, Molinari was the first advocate of *anarcho-capitalism* – economic freedom without government. A Belgian-born admirer of **Frédéric Bastiat**, he became the leading advocate of laissez-faire in nineteenth-century France. Over a long life as a journalist and economist, he promoted the ideas of free trade, a minimal state, peace and abolitionism, and warned against protectionism, imperialism and militarism.

A thoroughgoing individualist, he even rejected the state monopoly on security that **John Locke** and other classical liberals all took for granted. Challenging the myth that government arises naturally for mutual protection, he asked why it should. On the contrary, he thought, if people and their property were menaced by others, they would simply hire expert providers to defend them. That is what they would do for any other good or service: why should security or other public services be different?

Monopoly, explained Molinari, rests on force. People will not pay monopoly prices unless they are forced to. A private monopoly might be replaced by a collective monopoly, but that still rests on force. And the most pernicious monopoly is security, since those who provide security already possess the coercive power to expand it and use it to enforce their interests on others. That is why a state monopoly of force does not suppress war, but *promotes* it.

People may secure some parliamentary control over the use of force, but it remains a monopoly underpinned by coercion. Constitutional plunder is still plunder – which undermines people's faith in their rulers and in their right to govern. But social arrangements can also arise through utility rather than terror. People needing protection will strike bargains with those who can provide it, and will gain the benefits of efficiency and value for money. These ideas greatly influenced **David Friedman**.

[66] Herbert Spencer (1820–1903): English sociologist and polymath. **Key ideas:** Freedom and progress; evolution of harmonious societies; political rights; universal suffrage; non-cooperation with bad governments. **Key works:** *Social Statics* (1851); *The Man Versus the State* (1884).

Home-educated, Spencer worked as a railway civil engineer before joining *The Economist*. He shared the magazine's support for free trade, laissez-faire and limited government, but his interests turned towards human social psychology. He speculated on evolutionary theory some years before Charles Darwin (1809–1882) published *The Origin of Species* (1859). But, unlike Darwin, he did not grasp the principle of natural selection, believing that *acquired* characteristics were passed on (a mistake now known as Lamarckism). He also extended evolutionary theory to psychology and culture; and where Darwin saw evolution as a continuing process with no ultimate goal, Spencer imagined our evolutionary progress towards 'the perfect man in the perfect society'. Human societies, he suggested, had evolved from being simple, hierarchical and warlike into being complex, cooperative and industrial. As a result, individual human beings were evolving into less aggressive creatures.

It was Spencer, not Darwin, who coined the phrase 'survival of the fittest'. This led to him being dismissed as a 'Social Darwinist' – an impression reinforced by other sweeping remarks, such as: 'The ultimate effect of shielding men from the effects of folly, is to fill the world with fools'. But though he was a social evolutionist, Spencer distanced himself from Social Darwinism, pointing out that the 'fittest' was not necessarily the 'best'.

Spencer was in fact a *liberal utilitarian*. Evolution, he explained in *The Principles of Ethics* (1879–93), promotes useful character traits such as cooperation. This benefits the survival and welfare of the group – and therefore the survival and welfare of the individuals within it. Like **John Stuart Mill**, he believed that free societies would progress faster than others: allowing people to experiment gives evolution more material to work on, he explained. Individual liberty was also associated with the ideas of moral equality, equal justice, and the right to life and liberty, which again contributed to this successful evolution and therefore to the general happiness. These ideas become ingrained within individuals and society, giving rise to social institutions such as a liberal system of justice; and the societies that embrace them are the ones that flourish.

To Spencer, therefore, utility was a deeply liberal idea – not in conflict with but *based in* individual rights. In *The Man versus the State* (1884) he made a robust case for rights as the best defence against a damaging socialism. Because we are morally imperfect, he explained, we need *government* to defend our moral rights against violation by others; but we then need *political rights* to ensure that government does not itself violate our moral rights. This is crucial, since the impulse to interfere in others' lives is strong: 'Though we no longer presume to coerce men for their spiritual good, we still think ourselves called upon to coerce them for their material good: not seeing that the one is as useless and as unwarrantable as the other'.

Spencer considered several political rights that might limit the state. In *Social Statics* (1851), he advocated universal suffrage as an essential political right, though in the later *Principles of Ethics* (1879) he gave up on it as encouraging 'over-legislation'. Another right he originally saw as fundamental was the freedom to sever our connection with the state – to refuse paying in to it and in return not taking its benefits; but again in later life he concluded that this idea was impractical. And in *Social Statics* he thought private land ownership was incompatible with the principle of equal freedom, since it denied most people an essential resource; but in *Principles of Ethics* he once again abandoned this idea.

Though Spencer was prepared to amend his ideas on the basis of experience, he nonetheless remained true to his fundamental principle: that 'the liberty of each, limited by the like liberty of all, is the rule in conformity with which society must be organised'.

[67] John Elliott Cairnes (1823–1875): Irish political economist. **Key ideas:** Economic method; imperfect competition; economic deficiencies of slavery. **Key works:** *The Character and Logical Method of Political Economy* (1857); *The Slave Power* (1862).

The academically inclined son of an Irish brewer, Cairnes entered Trinity College Dublin. He studied law and was admitted to the bar, but did not practise, becoming more interested in economic issues. A prominent friend secured him the Chair of Political Economy.

His lectures were published as *The Character and Logical Method of Political Economy* (1857). The most important book on political economy since *Principles of Political Economy* (1848) by **John Stuart Mill** (of whom he was a disciple), it set out definitively the scope and method of classical economics. Political economy was a *science*, said Cairnes, and so was neutral about social systems and facts. But economists cannot experiment with their subject as natural scientists can with theirs, so economics could never be mathematical. Rather, it had to be deductive, drawing out principles from established facts.

Adroit with facts himself, his study of gold production in Australia and California led him to revive the *quantity theory of money* in what was the most important monetary analysis of his century. (**Milton Friedman** would revive the theory a hundred years later.) Likewise, Cairnes's factual analysis of slavery led him to highlight its disadvantages: slavery discouraged technological innovation, overworked the soil, stifled enterprise, and was ultimately unviable. His book, *The Slave Power* (1862), turned British opinion against the Confederacy in America.

In other work, Cairnes showed how, because of the class system, labour was not very mobile. The 'perfect competition' model therefore did not apply: society was more an assortment of non-competing industrial groups. These ideas stimulated the modern treatment of *imperfect competition*.

[68] Edward Atkinson (1827–1905): American anti-imperialist campaigner. **Key ideas:** Abolitionism; anti-imperialism; free trade. **Key work:** *Taxation and Work* (1892).

Forced to give up college through lack of funds, Atkinson became a successful entrepreneur in insurance and cotton manufacture. He also invented an improved stove, the Aladdin Cooker, and became a Fellow of the American Academy of Arts and Sciences. But he is remembered for combining the liberal ideas of anti-imperialism, abolitionism and free markets – ideas he pursued through his activism and through a vast output of papers and pamphlets on liberal political and economic themes including banking, free trade, competition, regulation and the evils of paper money.

Shocked by the expansionist, imperialist and colonialist policies of US presidents William McKinley (1843–1901) and Theodore Roosevelt (1858–1919) following the Spanish–American War, Atkinson helped found the American Anti-Imperialist League, and became its leading activist and pamphleteer, famously sending anti-imperialist pamphlets to the generals commanding US troops abroad.

He also supported a movement to assist escaped slaves, and raised money to support the armed insurrection of abolitionist John Brown (1800–1859). His death was reported as caused by 'a bout of indigestion, affecting the heart'.

[69] Josephine Butler (1828–1906): English social reformer and suffragist. **Key ideas:** Liberal feminism; emancipation; reform of prostitution laws. **Key work:** *The Education and Employment of Women* (1868).

As a social reformer, Josephine Butler helped improve female education and public health. She made *liberal feminism* a powerful force, confronting the policymakers and bringing difficult social issues into the public domain. As a campaigner, she developed new approaches to political action that would give strength to the later women's suffrage movement. Her written output includes some ninety books and pamphlets.

Butler was the daughter of a reformer and abolitionist who was a cousin of the prime minister, Earl Grey (1764–1845). When she married, her husband's work as a church teacher took her to Liverpool, where she became involved in family welfare issues. She rescued girls from the workhouse, giving them useful work, and campaigned against child prostitution, having discovered a slave trade in prostitutes as young as 12. From this experience, she led an ultimately successful movement to raise Britain's legal age of consent from 13 to 16.

Her second campaign was against the laws on contagious diseases. These laws, aimed at reducing the spread of sexual diseases among the army and navy, gave police the power to arrest women in ports and military towns and subject them to forced medical examination. If they resisted or showed signs of infection, they could be jailed. Butler argued that this encouraged police harassment of young women, and stripped half the population of their legal rights while doing nothing to halt the spread of infection by the other half. It was unusual for a woman to speak on such 'indelicate' subjects, at a time when women could not even vote; but Butler did not shy from arguing her case, even in public meetings. Again, her campaign raised awareness and ultimately succeeded.

In addition, Butler questioned women's 'natural' role as wife and mother, asking what that meant for the millions of unmarried women. She fought to expand female higher education, and helped push the University of Cambridge into establishing the women-only Newnham College.

8 THE MODERN ERA

By the middle of the nineteenth century, the world was reaping the rewards of expanding trade. American and Asian cotton fed Britain's vast textiles industry, with automation (based on steam and water power) slashing the price of clothes and fabrics that were then exported around the world. Steam power cut journey times and costs, both for goods and people. Raw materials such as wood and coal were being traded internationally, along with luxuries such as tea, coffee and exotic spices. Year by year, the trading world was becoming wealthier.

With wealth came the leisure to think – and do something – about society and politics. Britain had already ended slavery, reformed its Parliament and abolished the protectionist Corn Laws. But the liberals did not have the debate all their own way. Rapid industrialisation led to strains on families and social institutions, and on public infrastructure such as roads and rivers. There grew up a widespread feeling that we needed a new, *social* liberalism – not just leaving people alone, but *enabling* them to become free. Rapid change drove some campaigners towards new ideas such as anarchism (society without the state) and communism (collective ownership of resources), others back to a conservative past; while new economic and evolutionary theories took political and social thinking into yet other unexpected directions.

[70] Lord Acton [John Dalberg-Acton] (1834–1902): English Catholic historian and politician. **Key ideas:** Power corrupts; individual as the highest political end; liberty is not licence; importance of ideas in preserving liberty. **Key work:** *The History of Freedom and Other Essays* (1907).

Though Acton was more conservative than liberal, he has a place in the hearts of liberals for his remark: 'Power tends to corrupt and absolute power corrupts absolutely'.

Acton believed that Western civilisation was superior to others, having taken centuries to develop the idea that the individual was the highest value. The individual's liberty, therefore, 'is not a means to a higher political end. It is itself the highest political end'. It required protection 'against the influence of authority and majorities, custom and opinion'. Yet, as a committed Catholic, he was keen to distinguish *liberty* from *licence*: 'Liberty is not the power of doing what we like, but the right of being able to do what we ought'.

Acton applauded the federal structure of the US Constitution as a protector of personal freedom. He supported the Confederacy for its defence of states' rights against centralised government – which, he warned, could easily descend into tyranny if left unchecked.

But constitutions alone could not preserve freedom. Freedom depends on the ideas in which our institutions are rooted. Even liberal institutions degenerate over time if they do not live in the hearts and minds of individuals. Though the institutions of government may look liberal in form, he observed, they still do not necessarily defend liberty in practice.

[71] Auberon Herbert (1838–1906): English politician and individualist philosopher. **Key ideas:** Voluntaryism; protection the only role of government. **Key works:** *The Right and Wrong of Compulsion by the State* (1885); *The Voluntaryist Creed and a Plea for Voluntaryism* (1906).

A younger son of the Earl of Carnarvon, Herbert served in the British army and briefly became a Liberal Party Member of Parliament. Influenced by **Herbert Spencer**, he came to see free markets and voluntary cooperation as a better route to progress than politics:

> Refuse then to put your faith in mere machinery, in party organisations, in Acts of Parliament, in great unwieldy systems, which treat good and bad, the careful and the careless, the striving and the indifferent, on the same plan, and which on account of their vast and cumbrous size, their complexity, their official central management, pass entirely out of your control.

Herbert believed that government should be 'strictly limited to its legitimate duties', which were to 'protect the person and the property of the individual against force and fraud'. This, he argued, was the only justification for the use of force. Governments could not 'aggress upon' people's lives and property by imposing conscription, or compulsory education, or even taxation upon them. So the revenue needed for government's defence of liberty and property would have to be raised voluntarily:

> Force – whatever forms it takes – can do nothing for you. It can redeem nothing; it can give you nothing that is worth the having, nothing that will endure; it cannot even give you material prosperity ... Declare once and for good that all men and women are the only true owners of their faculties, of their mind and body, of the property that belongs to them; that you will only build the new society on the one true foundation of self-ownership, self-rule, and self-guidance...

Herbert gave speeches, wrote articles and published periodicals (one called *Free Life*) to promote his *voluntaryism*. He disliked being called an 'anarchist' because he accepted the need for a national government – albeit a very limited and voluntarily funded one. He even accepted that it would have to be a republican government steered by the majority. But he argued that being in the majority still does not confer any right to use force, except to repel force. The principle of self-ownership meant that 'neither an individual, nor a majority, nor a government can have rights of ownership in other men'.

Herbert thought that 'power is one of the worst, the most fatal and demoralising of all gifts you can place in the hands of men'. So it was with some justification that **Benjamin Tucker** called him 'a true anarchist in everything but name'.

[72] Henry George (1839–1897): American journalist and economist. **Key idea:** Land value tax. **Key work:** *Progress and Poverty* (1879).

Henry George began life as a ship's boy and a printer's assistant; but he taught himself economics, became a senior journalist and then, thanks largely to his book, *Progress and Poverty* (1879), an important economist and reformer.

George argued that most forms of taxation stifle growth: a tax on income, for example, was like slavery and would discourage people from creating and taking jobs. Likewise, import tariffs made prices high for consumers and protected established, monopolistic companies against competition. Only a *land value tax*, he thought, would be neutral in effect, because (as **David Ricardo** had noted) land was limited in quantity, so its 'production' would be unaffected by the tax.

George argued that people legitimately own what they create, but they do not create land, so natural resources in general should belong equally to the whole community. But beyond that, free markets and free trade were the best ways to raise the masses from poverty.

[73] Carl Menger (1840–1921): Austrian economist. **Key ideas:** Austrian economic theory; methodological subjectivism and individualism. **Key work:** *Principles of Economics* (1871).

Menger studied in Prague and Vienna before becoming a business journalist. In that role, he saw inconsistencies between the teaching of mainstream, 'classical' economics and the real-life workings of markets. So in 1867 he began writing a new approach, *Principles of Economics* (1871). By the age of just 33, he had become Chair in Economic Theory at the University of Vienna. He is remembered today as the founder of the Austrian School of Economics.

Menger thought classical economists were wrong to focus on whole collections of things, such as the total production of goods, or the total demand for them. This caused them to search vainly for mechanical linkages (such as 'equilibrium') between these totals. He called this *methodological collectivism*. What actually drives economic life, he maintained, is how individual people value individual goods, and how they act upon those values. Economics must therefore start from the values and actions of individuals – an approach he called *methodological individualism*.

A key part of this new method was *subjectivism*. Many economists thought that the value of a good was objectively measurable – its value was the amount of labour used to produce it. Menger countered that goods have no inherent value in themselves: *individuals* formed their own (and differing) valuations of them, depending on their specific needs and preferences. We now call this the *subjective theory of value*.

These approaches enabled Menger to develop the idea of marginal utility (now a central tenet of mainstream economics), solving the classical paradox of why water, a vital commodity, is valued less than diamonds, a largely useless one. He showed that value depends not just on the quality of the good itself, but on the quantity that is available to us.

Menger's individualism and subjectivism led him (and Austrian School followers such as **Ludwig von Mises** and **F. A. Hayek**) to reject interventionism: the economy was a process of mutual adjustments, not a machine to be tinkered with. Capitalism, he observed, encourages people to seek prosperity by serving others. Intervention disrupts that collaboration, creating mismatches that prompt calls for yet more intervention – fuelling the disruption even more.

[74] Bruce Smith (1851–1937): Australian politician and author. **Key ideas:** Conservative and liberal traditions; opposition to interfering government. **Key work:** *Liberty and Liberalism* (1887).

Born in the English port of Rotherhithe, close to central London, Smith's family migrated to Melbourne. He became a member of the New South Wales legislature before returning to run his father's shipping business, but in 1887 was disinherited after an argument. He went on to practise law and became a member of the Federal legislature (1901–1919). In business, he sought to reach agreement with the trade unions, and founded the Board of Conciliation in the state of Victoria – though he also founded the New South Wales and Victorian employers' associations.

At the age of 36, Smith wrote *Liberty and Liberalism* (1887), the first major study of liberalism published in Australia. A large and erudite book, it reviews the English, French and American liberal and conservative traditions in philosophy, politics and economics. With its long subtitle, *A Protest against the Growing Tendency toward Undue Interference by the State, with Individual Liberty, Private Enterprise and the Rights of Property*, Smith intended it as a counterblast to the 'new' liberals who were arguing for more 'meddling legislation' as he called it. Influenced by Spencer, voluntarism and the Manchester liberals, he argued throughout his life for free trade and laissez-faire. He was also a strong supporter of the women's movement and a critic of the White Australia policy.

[75] Benjamin Tucker (1854–1939): American publisher, individualist anarchist and egoist. **Key ideas:** Anarchism; property rights; personal freedom; ending regulation and state provision. **Key work:** *Liberty* (1881–1908).

Tucker came across anarchist ideas while studying at the Massachusetts Institute of Technology. He set about translating and publishing books and articles by radical thinkers such as the mutualist Pierre-Joseph Proudhon (1809–1865), the individualist anarchist Max Stirner (1806–1856), **Herbert Spencer** and **Lysander Spooner**. Between 1881 and 1908 he published the influential anarchist journal *Liberty*. In the course of this career, he developed his own strain of individualist anarchism.

Though he called himself a 'socialist', he was hostile to the idea of any collective authority. He thought that 'anarchistic workers' should own the fruits of their own labour, and be allowed to exchange it in a market unmarred by power and privilege. They would be at liberty to trade even in 'usury, rum, marriage, prostitution, and many other things which are believed to be wrong...'

But that meant ending several market 'monopolies' including bank regulation (which he said restricted competition and raised the cost of finance), land (which should confer title only on those who actually occupied and used it), tariffs (which raised the cost of imports to consumers) and patents (since ideas, unlike real property, should be freely accessible). He also objected to the state monopoly over defence and security, advocating a free market between competing providers.

In later life Tucker became more pessimistic at how the concentration of wealth, political centralisation and mass production were making society less individualist. But his ideas gave inspiration to **Murray Rothbard** and other *anarcho-capitalists* of the late twentieth century.

[76] Voltairine de Cleyre (1866–1912): American anarcha-feminist. **Key ideas:** Anarchism; criticism of gender roles and marriage. **Key work:** *Direct Action* (1912).

De Cleyre was a prolific poet, writer, essayist and speaker who opposed the authority of the state, the Church, and marriage. She is most remembered today for her essay *Direct Action* (1912), widely cited by protest movements.

Born into poverty in Michigan, de Cleyre's father named her after the French liberal **Voltaire**. Her Catholic education drove her to atheism, and she fell under the influence of liberals and anarchists such as **Thomas Paine, Thomas Jefferson, Mary Wollstonecraft** (about whom she wrote and lectured), **Lysander Spooner, Henry David Thoreau** and **Benjamin Tucker**, for whose anarchist journal *Liberty* she wrote articles. In later life she drifted towards mutualism, but ended as an 'anarchist without adjectives', seeing any non-violent system without government as defensible.

Her rejection of state authority was deepened by the tragedy in Chicago's Haymarket Square, where anarchists were protesting against the police having earlier fired into a crowd of strikers. A bomb was thrown and the police blamed the anarchists, arresting several, who were sentenced to death. De Cleyre saw this as judicial murder, by the authorities, of innocent political opponents.

De Cleyre was also a feminist. She argued that early socialisation forced children into unnatural gender roles, creating restrained girls and assertive boys. Marriage, in consequence, made women bonded slaves: men and women should instead arrange their lives as free beings. However, she regarded herself primarily as an anarchist, believing that the social and civil order – 'this mockery of order, this travesty upon justice' – oppressed both sexes. The solution was the empowerment of all humankind, not just women.

'I die, as I have lived', she wrote in her final days, 'a free spirit, an Anarchist, owing no allegiance to rulers, heavenly or earthly'.

[77] Albert J. Nock (1870–1945): American libertarian author. **Key ideas:** Radical anti-statism; anti-social nature of the state. **Key work:** *Our Enemy, The State* (1935).

A man of letters who is less well known today than he was in his time, Nock inspired a generation of individualists and individualist writings. The homeschooled son of a steel worker who served briefly as an ordained cleric, he became editor of the liberal, pro-capitalist and anti-war magazine *The Nation*, and a founding editor of *The Freeman*. In these roles, he discovered and encouraged **Suzanne La Follette**. Later, *Human Events, National Review* and the Intercollegiate Society of Individualists were established by admirers.

Nock's 'radical antistatist' approach – calling for a society based in natural liberty and free from the political influence of the state – was carried on by **Murray Rothbard** and other libertarians. While markets and society were not perfect, Nock insisted, the state cannot improve civilisation and morality. Indeed, it may make things worse.

The state, he explained in *Our Enemy, The State* (1935), was inherently anti-social, because it 'invariably had its origin in conquest and confiscation'. The only rights it recognised were those granted by itself. To reinforce this domination, the state made justice difficult and costly, and held itself above the law: for example, it banned monopolies while running them itself. And it suppressed economic freedom because there could be no other freedoms without that. 'In proportion as you give the state power to do things for you', he warned, 'you give it power to do things *to* you'. The weaker the state was, the less power it would have to commit crimes – or start wars, which encouraged the evils of 'collectivisation, imperialism, nationalism and flag-worship'.

Nock blamed the US administrations of the 1920s for creating the Great Depression by piling credit on credit – followed by yet more 'pump priming' to counter the slump. He also denounced the 'New Deal' remedy as a pretext to extend government power and control – which, he warned, would prove permanent, despite being advertised as temporary.

He opposed centralisation, regulation, income tax, state welfare and compulsory education. State education, he complained, promoted a servile reverence for the state and a uniformity of ideas, conduct, lifestyle and beliefs: this was *training* rather than education. State welfare benefits were a fraud, with people made to think it was others, not themselves, who were paying the cost. And income tax had perverse results that were so commonplace that they were not even noticed.

Nock was pessimistic about the future of liberty, seeing himself as a 'remnant' – one of a small minority who understood the nature of state and society, but who would have no influence until the present system collapsed. Until then, he suggested, the best course was to surround oneself with great ideas and people who share them.

9 THE FREE ECONOMY AND SOCIETY

The late nineteenth and early twentieth centuries brought many developments in the emerging field of economics. As the confidence of economists increased, many began to see their discipline as the equal of the natural sciences. They came to believe that economists could predict, plan and shape economic affairs just as physicists had done with natural phenomena. Liberals faced the new challenges of 'scientific' socialism, central planning and state control of industry.

Liberalism, with its emphasis on individualism and laissez-faire, seemed increasingly old-fashioned and ir-relevant. Russia, China and other countries went commu-nist – with the full support of Western intellectuals, who saw them as exciting, bold, rational models for their own countries. And in the West, the same collectivism that won World War II would now 'win the peace' – providing wel-fare, housing, health, education and employment for all.

The liberals' critiques of socialism did little to slow down its march or counter its emotional attractions. The few remaining liberals gathered in safe havens such as **F. A. Hayek**'s Mont Pelerin Society to keep the flame alive. All they could do was to wait, until the dire consequences that they predicted of the collectivist experiment actually became plain. Meanwhile, they would work on developing new liberal approaches that were more in tune with the realities of a rapidly changing world, so that when events did turn, they would be ready.

[78] Ludwig von Mises (1881–1973): Austrian economist. **Key ideas:** Austrian economics; case against regulation; impossibility of socialist calculation; business cycles; hard currency. **Key works:** *The Theory of Money and Credit* (1912); *Socialism* (1922); *Liberalism* (1927); *Human Action* (1949).

Mises was one of the most significant liberal economists and political scientists of his time. He became the leading figure of the Austrian School of economics – influencing many others, including **F. A. Hayek** and **Murray Rothbard**.

Mises made a robust case for laissez-faire, arguing that free markets, the division of labour and free exchange were the only economic arrangement that brought sustainable prosperity. As soon as governments started *hampering* the market economy, he insisted, they set off waves of dislocation, creating surpluses and shortages that required further interventions to repair. These in turn had yet other unwelcome results that demanded further action, until in the end the whole market process was smothered. This in turn would erode the foundations of the liberal social order, since freedom depended on private property and free trade. Governments should therefore not embark on intervention at all.

Mises started life (like **F. A. Hayek**) as a mild socialist. But he came across **Carl Menger**'s *Principles of Economics* (1871), which fundamentally changed his outlook. He took up, developed and systematised Carl Menger's *methodological individualism* and *subjectivism*. Mainstream economists, he argued, failed because of their *collectivist* approach. In trying to copy the success of the natural sciences, they searched for mechanical linkages between measures such as aggregate demand, aggregate supply and the price level, hoping to use that knowledge to plan more 'rational' economic systems. But there were in fact no scientific relationships between these things, which were merely statistical groupings. Real, individual things might affect one another, he argued, but statistics never could. Indeed, by lumping together very different goods and services – apples, bricks, haircuts, cheese, shoes, glassware, cash registers and bus journeys – these aggregates merely *conceal* what is really going on underneath. It is absurd to speak of the price 'level', for example, when there are in reality only millions of individual prices, each rising or falling from moment to moment.

What actually drove economic life, said Mises, were the specific values and actions of millions of diverse individuals. But human values cannot be measured and calculated in equations. People react to economic changes in different ways: a rise in the price of sugar may cause some people to panic buy it, but others to cut down their consumption. And we cannot predict how they will react tomorrow.

By applying this idea systematically across various economic phenomena, Mises produced many fresh insights. To mainstream economists, for example, money was a lifeless *medium of exchange*. To Mises, money was an *economic good* – valued, like other things, for its usefulness. Its price (i.e. its *purchasing power* in terms of other goods) was determined by the same market forces that determine the price of any other economic good. The amount that people chose to keep handy (in their wallets or bank accounts, say) depended on how useful they thought it would be in making future purchases. The more useful they considered it, the higher its purchasing power rose; the less useful, the lower its purchasing power fell. That insight on individual values and actions told us much about inflation that mainstream economists, with their *methodological collectivism*, could never understand.

Business cycles were another case in point. Mises and Hayek traced these boom–bust episodes back to the easy-credit policies by which central banks tried to stimulate economic growth. Sadly, the *false signal* of low interest rates fuelled borrowing, spending and investment – but the same low interest rates discouraged people from saving. Without savings, the boom would run out of funds: businesses would have to abandon their investment plans, and people would be thrown out of work. Paper money, thought Mises, gave the banks far too much discretion to set off such disastrous cycles. Only a hard currency, such as gold, could restrain them.

Applying the same method in *The Theory of Money and Credit* (1912), Mises also gave us a better understanding of the nature of capital and interest. *Interest*, he maintained, was not some automatic 'return' on saving. Rather, it depended on how the individuals involved valued the *future* – whether they thought it worth giving up consumption today in order to produce the fishing nets, ploughshares and machines that might boost production tomorrow. This trade-off showed the crucial importance of *time*, and how people value it, in all economic calculations. But time – and values – were overlooked in the mainstream approach.

And similarly, by focusing only on statistical totals, the mainstream economists mistakenly treated *capital* as something uniform. But precisely *which* capital goods people invested in – the *capital structure* – was crucial, Mises insisted. However large or small the total happened to be, investment in the wrong capital goods – *malinvestment* – was debilitating. Only the individualist method revealed this.

In *Socialism* (1922), Mises argued that economic calculation becomes impossible when markets cease to exist. Under state ownership, productive inputs such as factories and equipment are never bought or sold, so are never priced. Without input prices, we cannot know which of many possible production processes is the cheapest. So we have no rational way to choose between them. Inevitably, over-expensive processes will be chosen, and resources wasted. The market economy, by contrast, puts competitive pressure on producers to choose the most cost-effective methods – thus reducing waste and preserving vital resources intact for other purposes.

In response to this devastating criticism, socialist economists proposed 'market socialism', in which resources
would be allocated 'as if' markets existed; but Mises re-
torted that market socialism could work only when there
were real market prices for it to copy; the wider that socialism spread, the less was it able to plan production rationally. Socialism would simply smother itself.

[79] Frank Knight (1885–1972): American economist and
moralist. **Key ideas:** Economic freedom basic to other
freedoms; markets and politics are both flawed; interventionism can do more harm than good. **Key work:** *Risk,
Uncertainty and Profit* (1921).

Frank Knight was a founder of the Chicago School of economics, which included his students **Milton Friedman**,
George Stigler and **James Buchanan**. He was also a founder member (along with Friedman, Stigler, **Ludwig von
Mises** and **F. A. Hayek**) of the Mont Pelerin Society, the
spearhead of the liberal revival after World War II.

Knight began student life studying for the clergy, but
ended it with an economics doctorate from Cornell. His
classic thesis, *Risk, Uncertainty and Profit* (1921), high-
lighted the vital role of entrepreneurs in steering new
products and processes through the *uncertainty* of events
that cannot be anticipated at all, and the *risk* of events that
can be anticipated, but whose scale and impact cannot be
accurately predicted.

He argued that economic freedom was basic to our other
freedoms. Freedom was not only an end in itself, but a means

to achieve other values. Free markets were an essential part of that freedom, and were better than other systems at managing people's conflicting ambitions. But markets were never perfect: laissez-faire policies, he warned, would simply leave their faults uncorrected. Nor could markets solve all social, moral and personal conflicts – which meant that government had to set limits to freedom.

That, however, would create political conflicts. And since it was impractical for people simply to leave a political society they disagreed with, compromise was needed. This in turn would require democratic debate and representative government to achieve. But democracy is a battle between competing interests, just like markets, and has many of the same failings.

It is precisely because politics and economics are *both* flawed, Knight concluded, that even well-intended political interventions in markets can easily make things worse. We should not intervene unless there is a clear problem and a clear prospect of success. Nor should we hesitate to act if this is the case. But we need to be acutely aware that not every social problem has a solution.

[80] Isabel Paterson (1886–1961): Canadian-American journalist, novelist, critic and anarchist philosopher. **Key ideas:** Creativity stifled by laws; regulations promote powerful businesses and create monopolies. **Key work:** *The God of the Machine* (1943).

Isabel Paterson, **Rose Wilder Lane** and **Ayn Rand** became known as the three 'mothers' of American libertarianism.

Paterson, one of nine children born to a family in Ontario's remote Manitoulin Island, was largely (like Lane) self-taught, and in her teens took various low-paid jobs, including waitress, bookkeeper and stenographer. She married in 1910 but (like Lane, again) separated less than a decade later. She took writing and editorial jobs in the US, and was quickly promoted, becoming an influential literary critic, known for her acerbic wit. She also wrote westerns and historical novels.

Her book *The God of the Machine*, published in 1943 (the same year as Lane's *The Discovery of Freedom*), was a founding text of individualist philosophy. In it, she asked why some countries remain prosperous while others stagnate. Her answer was that the economic and legal principles of the former allow individual creativity to flourish. The Roman Empire expanded, she argued, not because of its military might, but because of its open institutions, commerce and social mobility, which set creativity free.

According to Paterson, monopolies arose largely out of privileges bestowed by governments. Antitrust laws did not end this. Indeed, when cheap producers can be accused of 'predatory pricing', costlier ones of 'price gouging' and those who charge the same of 'price fixing', it is the established, politically connected firms which can best turn the argument to their own advantage.

We should judge policies by their results, not their intentions: 'Most of the harm in the world is done by good people, and not by accident, lapse, or omission', she wrote. 'It is the result of their deliberate actions, long persevered in, which they hold to be motivated by high ideals toward virtuous ends'.

At the *New York Herald Tribune*, where Paterson wrote a regular column, she met **Ayn Rand**. They became friends and promoted each other's books, but broke up in 1948 over an argument. Shortly afterwards, Paterson was eased out of the *Tribune*: her calls for less government in social, welfare and economic matters were against the mood of the times. But by then she had made enough money to re- fuse to take benefits from the recently established Social Security (America's national pension system), which she described as a 'swindle'. (Lane followed suit, though Rand famously and controversially decided to take the benefits.)

[81] Rose Wilder Lane (1886–1968): American journalist, novelist and political theorist. **Key ideas:** State erosion of individual liberties; creativity of free people. **Key work:** *The Discovery of Freedom* (1943).

Rose was born in South Dakota, the daughter of Laura In- galls Wilder (1867–1957), author of the *Little House on the Prairie* books. Largely self-educated, she married in 1909 and took a series of clerical, writing and newspaper jobs. In 1915 she joined the *San Francisco Bulletin*, where she was soon valued as a skilled editor and writer. By 1918, her marriage had ended and she started writing novels and biographies, as well as short stories, articles and reviews in national journals such as *Harper's* and the *Saturday Evening Post* – eventually becoming America's highest-paid female writer.

In the course of extensive travels in America and Europe, she recanted her youthful socialism, having seen at first hand the tyranny of Soviet Russia and bureaucratic oppression in interwar Europe. Economic planning, she concluded, was no friend of liberty and prosperity:

> I am now a fundamentalist American; give me time and I will tell you why individualism, *laissez-faire* and the slightly restrained anarchy of capitalism offer the best opportunities for the development of the human spirit. Also I will tell you why the relative freedom of human spirit is better – and more productive, even in material ways – than the communist, Fascist, or any other rigidity organized for material ends.

Much of her subsequent writing highlights her growing dismay at the state's erosion of individual liberties. Her most enduring book, *The Discovery of Freedom* (1943), shows the importance of individuals who advance progress by acting against majority opinion – and how state planning and regulation thwarts them. She became a friend and mentor to **Ayn Rand**, who took up this idea.

Lane attacked the New Deal as 'creeping socialism'. She campaigned against zoning laws as infringing property rights, and gave up a column and editorial job to avoid paying taxes for Social Security, calling this pay-as-you-go pension system a 'Ponzi fraud'. She maintained an unshakeable faith in the creative power of free individuals, writing (at a time when the world population was less than a third of its present figure): 'The revolution is only beginning. When all living men know that men are born free, the energy of twenty-two hundred million human beings will be released upon this earth. A hundred million have made America. What will twenty-two hundred millions do?'

[82] Walter Eucken (1891–1950): German economist.
Key ideas: Ordoliberalism and the German economic miracle. **Key work:** *The Order of Economics* (1937).

Eucken is remembered as the father of *ordoliberalism*, the German neoliberal ideas that helped reverse post-war economic stagnation and created the German 'economic miracle' (*Wirtschaftswunder*).

Born into an academic family, Eucken studied economics and became a professor in Berlin, and then in Freiburg. There, he helped create the Freiburg School of economics, which was broadly liberal but saw government as having a legitimate role in restraining markets so as to prevent undesirable social consequences. In the late 1930s, Eucken and other colleagues who opposed Hitler built on their Freiburg School principles to set out a post-war economic strategy that would replace the central planning of the Nazis with a more liberal competitive system. Their resistance to Nazism saw Eucken arrested, and others executed.

Nevertheless, *ordoliberalism* would later shape post-war economic policy and unleash the 'miracle'. Under Eucken's approach, the state would provide a liberal economic framework based in property rights, open markets and monetary stability. This would not be laissez-faire, which Eucken believed would produce cartels and an over-concentration of corporate power. Rather, the state would promote competition and limit the power of companies.

Ludwig Erhard (1897–1977), Economic Director of the important British–American sectors of post-war Germany, adopted the *ordoliberal* approach, abolishing wage and price controls and introducing a more stable currency (the Deutsche Mark). Within a few years, Germany was enjoying its 'miracle' recovery.

[83] Suzanne La Follette (1893–1983): American libertarian feminist journalist. **Key idea:** Economic basis of libertarian feminism. **Key work:** *Concerning Women* (1926).

La Follette was raised on a farm in the western US. The daughter of a US congressman whose cousin was also a senator, she worked briefly on Capitol Hill. Moving to New York, she met **Albert Jay Nock**, who recruited her for his short-lived journal *The Freeman*.

Nock encouraged La Follette to write *Concerning Women* (1926), the most significant book on libertarian feminism since **Mary Wollstonecraft**'s *Vindication of the Rights of Women* (1792). It argued that the subjection of women, like slavery, was rooted in economic institutions backed by the state. The state, through labour legislation, minimum wages and restrictive laws on prostitution, birth control and illegitimacy, put women at such an economic disadvantage that, for most, marriage was the only option. But marriage laws compounded the disadvantage by giving all the rights to the male partner, making divorce difficult, and leaving women dependent and without property.

La Follette maintained that economic equality for women, and indeed for any class or group, would come only when *everyone* was treated equally. The issue was not to spare women from the control of men, but to remove *all* violations of individual rights by privileged and powerful elites. Moreover, without economic freedom, she insisted, political and social freedom would remain an illusion. Economic freedom was more important than political equality and votes for women. Real emancipation, for all groups, implies the destruction of the state.

In the 1930s, La Follette worked to exonerate Leon Trotsky (1879–1940) from treason charges against him by the Soviet dictator Joseph Stalin (1878–1953). She later revived *The Freeman* as a libertarian, anti-statist literary magazine, *The New Freeman*, and in later life became the first managing editor of *National Review*.

[84] F. A. Hayek (1899–1992): Anglo–Austrian economist and political scientist. **Key ideas:** Business cycle theory; critique of planning; limits to human information; errors of rationalism; spontaneous order. **Key works:** *The Road to Serfdom* (1944); *The Constitution of Liberty* (1960); *Law, Legislation and Liberty* (1973).

Hayek was one of the most intellectually fertile liberal thinkers. Born into an academic family with diverse interests, he went on to write about economics, philosophy, politics, psychology and the history of ideas. His Nobel

Prize reflected this range, being awarded for his work on business cycles and his explanation of spontaneous orders in human society.

Hayek's 1944 wartime critique of socialist planning, *The Road to Serfdom*, which showed how easily social democracy could morph into totalitarianism, brought him popular fame. Soon after, he founded the Mont Pelerin Society, a forum for liberal ideas that influenced a whole generation of intellectuals and informed the policies of Margaret Thatcher (1925–2013), Ronald Reagan (1911–2004) and the new Eastern European leaders who emerged after the fall of the Berlin Wall.

After wartime service, Hayek was hired as an economist by **Ludwig von Mises**, and in 1927 the pair set up an institute to explore boom–bust cycles. They concluded that these cycles were caused by central banks setting interest rates too low – encouraging excessive borrowing, investment and spending. But low rates also discouraged saving, and when funds dried up, investments had to be abandoned and people were thrown out of work. Hayek later suggested that the best preventative was *competition in currency* – so that people could switch easily to sounder currencies.

In the 1930s, Hayek came to Britain, becoming professionally famous – partly through his disputes with John Maynard Keynes (1883–1946). Keynes advocated government spending to boost the economy; Hayek argued that this would bring only inflation, disruption and debt.

But Keynesian ideas won the day, and Hayek turned more to social and political philosophy. His key insight was the concept of *spontaneous order*, which he traced back to **Adam Ferguson**, **Adam Smith** and others. Human and animal societies, he observed, show obvious regularities. Yet nobody planned the society of bees or human language or the operations of markets. They came about naturally and spontaneously, and evolved and persisted simply because they were useful. Spontaneous orders emerged when we followed certain regular ways of acting – *rules* such as the rules of grammar, or of markets. Often we could not articulate the rules, nor even realise we were following them. But these regularities contained an evolved wisdom – the information or knowledge that allows us to thrive.

The relationship between the individual rules and the overall outcome was complex: and since we were ignorant of how such orders work, warned Hayek, it was folly to believe that we could easily improve on them. Economic planning, for example, was not merely a problem of collecting and crunching data to find the best outcome. The planner cannot even access the information necessary for the decision – because that information is dispersed, partial, rapidly changing and impossible to transmit. To know what to produce, the planner would need to know people's wants and *values* – which cannot be measured or communicated. Indeed, the dismal failure of central planning through the decades was ample evidence of how impossible the task was. And yet the spontaneous market order processed all this dispersed and partial information, at every local level, from moment to moment. We had no need to identify some shared objective: markets reconcile people, like buyers and sellers, who have different objectives and values. (In fact, the more disagreement about what people value, the easier it is for them to cooperate through trade.) Market systems can therefore grow far larger and more complex than planned orders.

We did not design this system, said Hayek: rather, we stumbled upon it. When people first started bartering and swapping goods, they did not know it would grow into a worldwide system of cooperation through trade and commerce. But when they did barter and exchange, *prices* began to emerge, and prices contain all the information needed for the system to work. We did not need to know *why* people have come to value something, or what use they found for it, or why they wanted more: a rising price said it all. Then, the prospect of profit drew people's energy into supplying that good, steering resources towards their most valued uses and away from wasteful ones – and reconciling the diverse ambitions of different people, quite automatically.

Another aspect of this automatic system was constant improvement. Facing competition from others, suppliers constantly tried to differentiate their products. Through constant innovation and customer selection, products became better and cheaper. Markets and competition were never 'perfect', but were an evolutionary *process* of differentiation, discovery and improvement.

Hayek saw freedom as critical to the operation of spontaneous orders. When planners try to achieve some preconceived outcome by compelling us to act in certain ways, they disrupt our rule-guided behaviour, lose the wisdom of the rules and put the whole order at risk. Also, spontaneous social and economic orders needed innovations and new ideas to work on in order to evolve, grow and strengthen (as **John Stuart Mill** observed). Free people were creative and innovative people; when we restricted their freedom we had less to fuel the evolutionary process.

Freedom, to Hayek, meant minimising coercion. Society was built on rules, not commands, and we gave the state limited coercive power only to prevent people breaking the rules – not to force them to act in particular ways. To prevent the abuse of such power, we needed government to be constrained by rules too. Hayek called this the *rule of law*: laws had to be known and certain, applicable equally to all, not be retrospective, and (as **Joseph Priestley** had put it earlier) leave us the largest *private sphere* possible.

Hayek saw *justice* as the rules that enabled the social order to work. We could not invent the rules of justice: we had to discover them through trial and error. What people call 'social justice' was quite different – not a set of rules but a preconceived social outcome. Achieving that outcome meant treating people differently; and once we began to do that, we were on the road to serfdom, with no obvious stopping point. But 'social justice' was a mirage anyway, because there was no agreement about how such redistribution should be made. Hayek argued that 'social justice' would dissolve into competing interest groups lobbying for state support.

To Hayek, the socialist vision of society was a mistake. A liberal government would merely create the conditions needed for the social order to function. *Law* was our attempt to *discover* the rules of justice; governments should not imagine that they could *legislate* the running of an entire society. Nor should they think that a democratic majority allows them to exceed their proper role. Rather, they should be constrained by a constitution that ensured that people were indeed treated equally, such that special interests could not be indulged, and the talent of free people could be released.

[85] Karl Popper (1902–1994): Anglo-Austrian philosopher. **Key ideas:** Historicist root of authoritarianism; false science and intolerance; importance of toleration. **Key works:** *The Poverty of Historicism* (1936); *The Open Society and Its Enemies* (1945).

Popper was a prominent philosopher of science, who also made important contributions to political philosophy. A Marxist in his youth in Vienna (where he was a friend of **F. A. Hayek**), he soon rejected the Marxists' dogmatism and use of violence. For some years he remained an idealistic socialist, but came to reject egalitarianism as incompatible with the key political value of freedom. Though he continued to argue for the state's role in solving social problems, his anti-authoritarianism and defence of individualism, reason, toleration, peace and freedom in an 'open society' establish his liberal credentials.

Popper produced major critiques of fascism, nationalism, collectivism and central planning. Much of this was based on his philosophy of science. He held that all supposed 'knowledge' was in fact mere *theory*, which new evidence might later prove false. Dictators' claims to know 'certain truth' were therefore hollow: useful ideas prospered only in *non*-authoritarian, 'open' societies. This made tolerance essential. But paradoxically (and controversially):

> Unlimited tolerance must lead to the disappearance of tolerance. If we extend unlimited tolerance even to those who are intolerant, if we are not prepared to defend a tolerant society against the onslaught of the intolerant, then the tolerant will be destroyed, and tolerance with them.

Popper argued that the flawed methods of the social sciences – focusing on groups rather than individuals – licensed despotic leaders to make individuals subservient to their own political idea. They also suggested that events were determined not by individuals but by historical 'laws' – which again gave false authority to those (such as the Marxists) who claimed to understand them. But society was complex, no historical laws existed, and the unintended results of their conceit were always dire.

The political question, to Popper, was: 'How can we so organise political institutions that bad or incompetent rulers can be prevented from doing too much damage?' His answer was a system in which bad rulers could be ejected peacefully at elections. That is what justified a limited democracy: its precise form was far less important.

[86] Ayn Rand (1905–1982): Russian–American novelist and moralist. **Key ideas:** Truth found through objective thinking; ethics based on life; political principles founded

in ethics; creativity and progress require freedom.
Key works: *The Fountainhead* (1943); *Atlas Shrugged* (1957).

Ayn Rand, along with **Isabel Paterson** and **Rose Wilder Lane**, was one of the leading creators of modern American libertarianism – though she rejected the 'libertarian' label, calling herself a 'radical individualist' and a 'radical for capitalism'. Of the three, Rand is best remembered today, due in large part to her hugely influential novels *The Fountainhead* (1943), in which architect Howard Roark battles bureaucrats who compromise his radical vision, and *Atlas Shrugged* (1957), in which entrepreneurs respond to the stifling controls of a grasping government by closing down their businesses and setting up their own alternative society. Such is the popularity of these novels that, each year, they draw thousands of people (particularly young people) into the world of individualist ideas. A 1990s survey by the Library of Congress named *Atlas Shrugged* as the most influential book in the US, after the Bible.

The daughter of a Russian–Jewish pharmacist in St Petersburg, Rand was 12 when the Russian Revolution broke out. Her 'bourgeois' family fled to escape the fighting, and the Bolsheviks seized her father's business. The injustice of hard-working people being expropriated for the benefit of undeserving others would become a key theme in much of Rand's later writing. After the Revolution, Rand studied history and philosophy at the Petrograd State University, and then screenwriting at the State Institute for Cinema Arts. She obtained a visa to study the US film industry. In Hollywood she met and married an American actor, Frank O'Connor, and became a US citizen in 1931.

In New York, where her first play was showing, Rand became friends with **Isabel Paterson** and met **Ludwig von Mises**. She began writing the novels *We the Living* (1936), which described the suppression of the individual by the state in Soviet Russia, and *Anthem* (1938), set in a grim totalitarian future. Soon after, *The Fountainhead* (1943) became a word-of-mouth success and was made into a film starring Gary Cooper; it attracted a band of supporters – among them the future US Federal Reserve chairman Alan Greenspan (1926–), who met and discussed her ideas in a group ironically dubbed 'The Collective'. *Atlas Shrugged* (1957) became a bestseller despite unfavourable reviews, attracting millions to its core messages of individualism, laissez-faire capitalism and self-determination.

Rand's novels, along with her non-fiction works such as *For the New Intellectual* (1961) and *The Virtue of Selfishness* (1964), encapsulate her philosophical system, *Objectivism*, with its code of ethics built on *rational self-interest*. Like her philosophical heroes Aristotle (384–322 BC) and **Thomas Aquinas**, Rand derived her system from supposedly self-evident truths. She asserted that reality was objective, outside the human mind: consciousness was how we perceive things that exist; and reason was how we understand them. Reason was therefore essential to human existence, and was what defines us as human beings: when we neglected reason, we betrayed our humanity.

The highest moral purpose of rational individuals was *self-actualisation*. People should strive to achieve their own happiness – not instant gratification, but the rational, peaceful, long-term enhancement of their own lives and values. Rand condemned moral codes built on what she saw as irrational foundations, such as religion, collectivism and altruism. Peace and progress did not come from self-sacrifice, but from the pursuit of our own rational self-interest, the assertion of our own rights, and our respect for the similar rights of others. In her words: 'My philosophy, in essence, is the concept of man as a heroic being, with his own happiness as the moral purpose of his life, with productive achievement as his noblest activity, and reason as his only absolute'.

Rational human beings were responsible for their own actions – liable for the consequences of those actions and likewise entitled to their fruits. Nothing could legitimately be taken from them by force, since force is the antithesis of reason, and violates their rights. But among rationally self-interested individuals – like those in *Atlas Shrugged* who depart to create their own community – there would be no conflict, and no need for self-sacrifice. They would know that they could each benefit from the talents of other self-interested individuals through mutual agreement and exchange. Rand's heroes, in fiction and in reality, were people who asserted their individuality and who – not from altruism but through their own rational self-interest – invented technologies, created art and literature, advanced ideas and built businesses.

Rand argued that reason, the characteristic that defined our humanity, implied *egoism*, which in turn implied *capitalism*. She saw laissez-faire capitalism as the only economic system consistent with individual rights to life, liberty and property, and hence the only system likely to protect them, and the only system with any moral standing.

To further defend our natural rights and discourage violence, Rand advocated limited constitutional government, and condemned libertarianism for its anarchist tendencies. This created major rifts with other pro-freedom activists such as **Murray Rothbard**, and between objectivists themselves. Today, however, Rand's optimistic ideal, in which people do not follow the herd but lead rich, fulfilling, independent lives, draws huge numbers into freedom movements of every kind. As the saying goes, 'It usually begins with Ayn Rand'.

[87] Isaiah Berlin (1909–1997): Latvian–British philosopher. **Key ideas:** No single moral or political truths; positive and negative liberty. **Key works:** *Two Concepts of Liberty* (1958); *Four Essays on Liberty* (1969).

After the Russian revolution, Berlin's family fled to Britain, where he later won a scholarship to Oxford. The horrors inflicted by the communists in his boyhood home of Riga left him with a lifelong aversion to tyranny, and he became a leading defender of pluralism and toleration.

No single model or view or ideology, he argued, could encapsulate the huge diversity and dynamism of human ideas, values and history. There was no single true moral principle, no fixed standard by which action could be judged: life was a constant compromise between different and often conflicting values, such as freedom and equality. History was not determined by scientific laws or by great, impersonal forces as the Marxists thought: human life and human history were diverse and unpredictable.

In *Two Concepts of Liberty* (1958), Berlin distinguished between *positive* and *negative* liberty. Negative liberty, exemplified in the work of **John Locke** and **John Stuart Mill**, upheld people's right to act without restraint. Positive liberty argued that people could not be truly free unless they could shape their own destiny and achieve self-actualisation. While Berlin saw merit in both concepts, and while we have a natural desire to help others to live fulfilled lives, he feared that the positive freedom idea was being used by ideologues to undermine, not supplement, the negative freedom that was the cornerstone of classical liberalism. He explored this theme further in *Four Essays On Liberty* (1969).

[88] Ronald Coase (1910–2013): English Nobel economist and legal theorist. **Key ideas:** Transaction costs; property rights and market outcomes. **Key works:** *The Nature of the Firm* (1937); *The Problem of Social Cost* (1960).

One of the few economists to have a theorem named after him, Coase's time at the London School of Economics convinced him to become an economist rather than a lawyer. Nevertheless, his work focused on how laws and institutions affect market outcomes. He became editor of the *Journal of Law and Economics*, and won a Nobel Prize for his insights in two major articles.

The Nature of the Firm (1937) showed how the size and structure of firms depended on *transaction costs* – such as the *search costs* of finding suppliers and customers, *bargaining costs*, and the costs of *enforcing contracts*. Technology could dramatically alter these costs, leading to completely new market structures (as the growth of today's web-based 'sharing economy' shows).

In *The Problem of Social Cost* (1960), Coase outlined his theorem that there could be no market failure in 'perfectly competitive' markets. Markets failed when property rights were not well defined, which raised transaction costs (such as the cost of legal disputes). Even so, the parties would seek out the cheapest mutually beneficial solution: a noisy workshop, for example, might pay cash compensation to its neighbours rather than fight costly lawsuits. The solution to market failure, therefore, is not necessarily regulation, but to clarify property rights, which cuts transaction costs and enables market solutions to emerge. This conclusion has greatly influenced policy debates on environmental issues, from forestry through water management to the allocation of broadcast spectrum, and informed the work of **Elinor Ostrom** on managing 'common pool' resources with minimal government intervention.

[89] Milton Friedman (1912–2006): American economist. **Key ideas:** Quantity theory of money; licensing benefits only producers; school vouchers; the case against lifestyle regulation; unintended consequences of economic intervention. **Key works:** *Capitalism and Freedom* (1962); *Free to Choose* (1980).

Friedman was a Nobel Prize–winning economist whose work on professional licensing and on inflation policy convinced him that government regulation and economic management were counterproductive.

For most of his professional life, however, such liberal views were in the minority: from the 1930s to the 1980s, the world economy was dominated by a faith in government planning and control. But Friedman was a particularly able and persuasive communicator of liberal ideas. Through his book *Capitalism and Freedom* (1962) and his TV series and book *Free to Choose* (1980) – both written with his wife Rose – millions of people came to learn about the potential of free markets, open trade, freedom and capitalism. When the old centralist thinking was finally discredited by its mounting failures, it was these ideas that replaced them – becoming part of the everyday life of billions of the world's citizens. 'There are very few people who have ideas that are sufficiently original to materially alter the direction of civilization', concluded the former US Federal Reserve Chairman Alan Greenspan. 'Milton is one of those very few people'.

Friedman was born in Brooklyn, New York, to Hungarian Jewish immigrant parents. His father took work as he could get it, while his mother sewed garments in a New York sweatshop. (Friedman would later explain to his *Free to Choose* television audience how such workplaces provided the poorest with a vital step on the ladder to self-improvement.) The family made a point of speaking English at home, and Milton excelled at school, winning university places at Rutgers and Chicago, where he studied under **Frank Knight**.

After various government appointments, Friedman joined his friend George Stigler (1911–1991) – later a Nobel laureate himself – at the University of Minnesota. They collaborated on *Roofs or Ceilings?* (1946), a pungent repudiation of rent controls – which, they argued, made landlords less willing to maintain and rent out their property, reducing both the quality and supply of accommodation. Around the same time, Friedman published *Income from Independent Professional Practice* (1945), showing that the chief beneficiaries from the regulation of professions (such as doctors, lawyers and accountants) were the practitioners themselves, rather than the public whom the regulation is supposed to protect. Because regulation restricted competition, customers ended up paying higher fees for a poorer service. Friedman's research on these and other issues convinced him that it was a matter of fact, not just theory, that capitalism produced greater economic efficiency (and more freedom and democracy) than the alternatives.

At Chicago, Friedman pitched into the fight against inflation – a particularly big problem in the post-war years. He strongly criticised the Keynesian orthodoxy that governments could manage inflation, boost employment and 'fine tune' economic growth through their taxing and spending policies. Friedman argued that to control inflation, governments had to restrain the *quantity of money* they put into circulation: no other tools would work. But such monetary policy was a very blunt instrument, so governments should just set up a sound framework and give up any idea of micro-managing things.

Capitalism and Freedom turned Friedman from an academic economist into a prominent public intellectual. The book addressed the great public issues of the day – economic policy, trade, education, discrimination, monopoly and poverty. Informed by the ideas of **John Stuart Mill** and **F. A. Hayek**, it argued that government intervention was illiberal and inefficient. It stressed the dignity of the individual and the role of diversity and variety in fuelling progress, and warned that concentrated power was the greatest threat to freedom and prosperity. Its policy prescriptions seemed impossibly radical at the time – introducing flat taxes, replacing Ponzi-style national pension systems with personal savings accounts, privatising mail services, ending conscription, decriminalising drugs. Yet within three decades, all these ideas – reprised in *Free to Choose* – had been implemented in several parts of the world.

Friedman's radical but evidence-based ideas, his straightforward and engaging explanations, and his cheerfulness in debate made him a media favourite, with frequent TV appearances. From 1966 to 1984 his regular *Newsweek* columns made him one of America's most prominent policy commentators: he used them to explain why minimum wages would hurt young blacks rather than help them; how current policy would produce inflation and recession at the same time (which mainstream economists thought impossible); how big business talked free markets but prospered on government favours; and much else.

Politicians and governments sought his advice: he helped the Nixon administration end a quarter of a century of fixed exchange rates and float the US dollar – though he resigned when Nixon introduced wage and price controls, which he predicted would have no impact on inflation and would only damage the economy.

After his retirement from Chicago, Friedman moved to California, where an enterprising film-maker proposed a multimillion-dollar documentary series in which he would present his own social, economic and political ideas. In each half-hour segment, Friedman simply explained his ideas in his usual fluent and candid way, unscripted, against the backdrop of world locations from America to the Far East. The series, *Free to Choose*, became an instant hit, and was screened around the globe. The book of the same name sold over a million copies. They brought Friedman's liberal ideas to a huge new audience, including politicians who would lead their countries after the collapse of the old thinking. 'The people of India and China may not realize it', commented Nobel economist **Gary Becker**, 'but the person they are most indebted to for the improvement of their situation is Milton Friedman'.

[90] James M. Buchanan (1919–2013): American economist and **[91] Gordon Tullock** (1922–2014): American political economist and legal theorist. **Key ideas:** Public Choice School; vested interests of electors, politicians and officials; government failure can be worse than market failure. **Key works:** *The Calculus of Consent* (1962); *The Vote Motive* (Tullock, 1976).

Buchanan and Tullock developed and promoted the Public Choice school of economics, which showed how the self-interest of voters, politicians and officials affected the nature and the efficiency of government decision-making. Buchanan received a Nobel Prize for his work on this subject.

Buchanan graduated from a local Tennessee college prior to wartime service. He went on to the University of Chicago, where the prominent economist **Frank Knight** converted him into a 'zealous advocate of the market order'.

Tullock took a law degree after his wartime service and joined the Foreign Service, working in various posts in the Far East, before teaching at Virginia Polytechnic Institute, where Buchanan later joined him. Pooling their talents in economics and public administration, the pair founded the Center for the Study of Public Choice (which later moved to George Mason University). They also collaborated on a pioneering book, *The Calculus of Consent* (1962), and created the journal *Public Choice*.

Public Choice theory challenged the naive assumptions of the prevailing 'welfare economists' who believed that *market failure* was common and needed government intervention to correct or offset it. But they assumed that public policy was made rationally and efficiently. Buchanan and Tullock, however, argued that rationality and efficiency in public decision-making was undermined at every point by self-interest and by the very nature of political institutions.

The outcome of elections, for example, was not objectively 'correct', but (as **Condorcet** showed) depended on the rules by which elections were conducted. Thus a *simple majority rule* made it easy to make decisions – but allowed just 50% + 1 to exploit the minority. A *qualified majority rule* (say, two-thirds or even unanimity) made decision taking harder – but protected minorities.

Elections, in any case, were not tests of the 'public interest', but contests of *competing* interests. Special interest groups, with a strong and shared interest in certain outcomes, had more dominance in elections than the general public, whose interests were diffused and moderate. They drove the political agenda, since politicians had to bid for their support in order to build the coalitions that would get them elected. This, said Tullock, encouraged *rent seeking*, where companies and groups campaigned for laws and regulations that would protect or profit them. Indeed, quite a small investment in lobbying could achieve huge financial returns for a special interest group.

Politicians also resorted to *logrolling* in order to get their measures through the legislature: but this 'you support my measure and I'll support yours' strategy meant that we ended up with more legislation than anyone really wanted. Lastly, the bureaucrats who enforced the laws also imposed their own motives on the process – for example, by over-complicating the regulations in order to build their own empires (or even to increase the opportunities for corruption).

The policy that emerged from this political process, concluded Buchanan and Tullock, may well be more damaging than the problem that it was meant to solve. We should remember that, while there is certainly *market failure*, there is *government failure* too.

[92] Murray Rothbard (1926–1995): American economist and political theorist. **Key ideas:** Anarcho-capitalism; free currency issuance. **Key works:** *Man, Economy and State* (1962); *For a New Liberty* (1973).

Rothbard was the leading architect of *anarcho-capitalism*. He regarded the state's monopoly on coercion as the greatest threat to individual liberty and public welfare. The state was 'the organization of robbery systematized and writ large', and laws that supposedly served the public good were created for the benefit of the 'bandit gang' that were the legislators. 'Taxation is theft, purely and simply', he wrote, 'even though it is theft on a grand and colossal scale which no acknowledged criminals could hope to match'.

Rothbard believed that everything provided by the 'monopoly system of the corporate state' could be better provided by private agencies. His anarcho-capitalist model envisaged the emergence of a variety of private protection agencies which would compete to offer people defence, policing and judicial services. This would end the state's monopoly on justice and the use of force. The state's coercive powers were immoral, thought Rothbard, because they gave the authorities a special privilege, violating the moral principle of equal treatment outlined by **Immanuel Kant**. For example, police officers who arrest drug users (violating their right to self-ownership) should be charged with kidnapping.

Rothbard fused these individualist views on rights and his anarchist rejection of the state with the laissez-faire economics of **Ludwig von Mises**. He saw the state's monopoly over currency issuance as a particularly destructive fraud, encouraging over-expansions of credit that create bubbles, booms and ultimately busts (as Mises and **F. A. Hayek** had explained). He consequently opposed central banks, fractional reserve banking and fiat money, which he dismissed as 'legalized counterfeiting' and embezzlement. Instead he advocated 100 per cent reserve banking, a voluntary gold standard, or competing private currencies. To him, 'Libertarianism holds that the only proper role of violence is to defend person and property against violence, and that any use of violence that goes beyond such defense is itself aggressive, unjust and criminal'.

10 CONTEMPORARY LIBERAL THINKERS

Liberals worked hard to keep the flame of liberalism alive after World War II and the decades that followed it. By the time that the baleful results of collectivism had become apparent, liberals had managed to develop a complete narrative on the shortcomings of socialism and the rationality of their own approach. They had also fashioned an impressive armoury of policy weapons to reinstate liberal economic and social policies: flat taxes, independent central banks, individual pension plans, private arbitration, deregulation of professions, privatisation of state industries, a capital owning democracy, and many more.

When the Berlin Wall fell in 1989, the Western public could see for themselves how dire life had been under communism. At last, a major threat to the very existence of liberal orders had been removed. But it had been replaced by other damaging threats – creeping regulation, populism, big government and a rising political class. Contemporary liberals were not short of problems to solve.

[93] Gary Becker (1930–2014): American economist.
Key idea: Application of economics to sociological issues.

Key works: *Human Capital* (1964); *The Economics of Discrimination* (1971).

A student of **Milton Friedman** who himself became a leading light of the Chicago school of economics, Becker received a Nobel Prize 'for having extended the domain of microeconomic analysis to a wide range of human behavior and interaction'. He applied economic principles, such as cost, benefit, price and investment, to diverse parts of human life that were traditionally regarded as matters of instinct, culture or emotion. This included education, crime, immigration, drugs, organ transplants and racial discrimination.

This analysis had important implications for public policy. For example, Becker showed that discrimination against minorities would be lower in more competitive markets. Laws designed to prevent firms discriminating were counterproductive: minority-only firms could compete by cutting costs and raising productivity and quality, leading to greater minority employment.

On crime, Becker argued that criminality was not always the product of some mental flaw, but that criminals made rational judgments about the gains from crime, compared with the chances of apprehension, conviction and punishment. Higher penalties and better enforcement would be more effective than the illiberal policy of greater surveillance.

Becker made big advances on *human capital*. Education, he showed, was not just a cultural asset, but a personal investment in oneself designed to boost one's productivity. So the demand for education could be analysed in economic, not just cultural, terms. Other human capital investments included training, work experience and even healthy lifestyles.

Becker applied his approach to democracy, specifically to vested interest groups' exploitation of others. As the rent seekers' gains increased, he argued, the losses to others rose exponentially. Eventually, squeezed beyond endurance, they would fight back violently – another argument for government, and its ability to regulate and grant favours, to be *limited*.

[94] Israel Kirzner (1930–): American economist.
Key ideas: Importance of entrepreneurship; importance of dynamics in economic theory. **Key works:** *Competition and Entrepreneurship* (1973); *Discovery, Capitalism and Distributive Justice* (1989).

The son of a Jewish scholar and rabbi, Kirzner was born in London. The family moved to Cape Town and then to New York, where he studied under **Ludwig von Mises**. He wrote on economic history and the ethics of markets, but his main contribution to liberal thinking is his work on the role and importance of entrepreneurship in the economic process.

In *Competition and Entrepreneurship* (1973), Kirzner criticised the neoclassical model of perfect competition as misleadingly static. Economics, he explained, was a *dynamic* process in which people adjusted their actions, and corrected their plans, in response to the changing actions of others. Traditional economic theory, focusing on 'equilibrium'

– and not on how markets might reach it – did not explain how people's economic actions were actually coordinated through this constant process of mutual adjustment.

A key part of this process was *entrepreneurship*, where people (not necessarily professional entrepreneurs, but ordinary people too) spotted gaps and mismatches in the market and then acted to fill and correct them. This in turn suggested that economic adjustment and coordination relied heavily on different individuals' local knowledge of market conditions – in contrast to the traditional assumption that everyone had 'perfect information'. It also reminded us that we must create the right conditions for this entrepreneurial spirit to thrive.

In *Discovery, Capitalism and Distributive Justice* (1989), Kirzner built on these ideas to provide an economic critique of 'social justice'. Entrepreneurs, he explained, constantly brought new resources into existence. It was impossible to achieve lasting equality through redistribution when the resources available to redistribute were always changing. And in any event, most people would agree that those who create something new are entitled to benefit from their innovation.

[95] Julian L. Simon (1932–1998): American business professor. **Key ideas:** How markets defeat scarcity; population as a positive resource. **Key works:** *The Ultimate Resource* (1981); *The Resourceful Earth* (1984).

Simon was the major critic of the conventional view that the world's resources were running out because of overpopulation and overexploitation. In reality, he argued, resources were getting cheaper. Rising wealth and better technology made it possible to exploit new resources; old resources could be recycled for reuse; and we constantly develop new alternatives to scarce resources.

The long-run prices of metals illustrated this point, argued Simon, because they were either stable or falling. He famously bet the American biologist Paul R. Ehrlich (1932–), one of the leading advocates of the conventional view, that any basket of five metals chosen by Ehrlich would be cheaper in a decade's time. They were: ten years later, unprompted, Ehrlich sent Simon his winnings, accompanied by a page of calculations.

Simon rejected the idea – popularised by Thomas Malthus (1766–1834) – that a rising population would create economic hardship. As he explained in *The Ultimate Resource* (1981) and other books, a rising population was not a drain on resources but in fact a solution to problems of scarcity, because people innovate. Human institutions, however, are as crucial in this as human minds, and the real problem was not too many people but too many restraints on their freedom.

A staunch advocate of markets, Simon suggested that airlines should offer travellers cash incentives to leave overbooked flights, instead of 'bumping' them at random – an idea eventually permitted by regulators and now used routinely in the airline business.

[96] Elinor Ostrom (1933–2012): American political scientist. **Key idea:** Spontaneous order in public goods management. **Key work:** *Governing the Commons* (1990).

Ostrom's Nobel Prize–winning work on how common resources are best managed began when she assisted her future husband, Vincent Ostrom, on his research into water resource management in southern California. Traditional economics suggested that common resources – such as fisheries, oil fields, grazing pasture, forests or water supplies – would be overexploited, unless state regulation prevented it. Ostrom's research, including studies in Africa and Nepal, showed that this is wrong. In fact, users often came up with their own methods of managing ecosystems long term – solutions that public policy interventions can easily dislocate.

Ostrom showed that societies develop diverse ways of protecting their ecosystems through *voluntary civil associations*. These rely on communication, trust and cooperation between users, backed up by effective monitoring, sanctions, and dispute resolution. Because local circumstances are critical, decisions are best made locally, not at the national level. Police services were an example. Cities often believed that small local police forces were wasteful and inefficient, and consolidated them into much larger units. But Ostrom showed that this neither saved money nor cut crime – quite the opposite, in fact.

Local, 'poly-centric' management may seem a hodge-podge, but it works, Ostrom concluded. The diversity both of local conditions and the people involved may be lost on higher government agencies. Poly-centric management enabled decisions to be made more quickly, and closer to the scene. We should be cautious, therefore, in placing too much trust in the state to manage our lives.

[97] Walter Williams (1936–): Afro-American economist and political theorist. **Key ideas:** Social, political and economic libertarianism; laissez-faire as the world's most moral and productive system; counterproductive nature of race laws. **Key work:** *The State Against Blacks* (1982).

In a large output of books and articles, Williams became a leading advocate of libertarian social, political and economic ideas. He took a robust line on many issues, such as the classical liberal principle of self-ownership. An essential part of ownership is that you can sell or give away what you own: therefore, said Williams, there should be no law against selling your own organs. He was equally direct on economic policy, saying that central banks' monopoly over a country's currency was effectively a licence to counterfeit.

Williams argued that free markets and laissez-faire were the most moral and productive system yet devised by humankind. Before capitalism, he explained, a minority of people acquired wealth by looting, plundering and enslaving others. Capitalism, by contrast, allowed everyone to acquire wealth by *serving* others.

Williams's research, presented in his book *The State Against Blacks* (1982), demonstrated that government interventions to boost minority employment (such as minimum wages and affirmative action) were counterproductive. For example, by raising the cost of employing people, minimum wages made employers more reluctant to take on minorities, who tended to have a poorer education and fewer skills. Such laws, he concluded, were worse than bigotry and discrimination – a criticism made all the more powerful by the fact that its author was black himself.

[98] Robert Nozick (1938–2002): American philosopher. **Key ideas:** The minarchist state; natural moral rights of individuals prior to legal institutions; no rational calculus for redistribution; no fixed stock of wealth to be shared out. **Key work:** *Anarchy, State and Utopia* (1974).

Nozick, who spent most of his professional life at Harvard, is best remembered for *Anarchy, State and Utopia* (1974). This book's uncompromising defence of the *minimal state* came as a shock to the academic establishment. The state, Nozick argued, is properly limited to protecting the individual rights of life, liberty, property and contract. It may not use its power to redistribute wealth or income, to direct people's lifestyles, to make them act morally, or to prevent them from self-harm. No other arrangement would be a moral state that would maximise the benefit of its individual members.

Individual rights are moral limits on how people can treat each other. They exist even before any 'social contract' might be agreed. We cannot morally violate them, whatever our motive. For example, we cannot force some people to sacrifice their property (e.g. by paying taxes) in order to promote the 'overall good of society' because there is no social entity with a good of its own to promote: there are only the individuals who comprise that community, who each have different interests. And as **Immanuel Kant** insisted, individuals are *ends* not *means*: we cannot abuse one person for the benefit of others. '[N]o moral balancing act can take place among us', concluded Nozick. 'There is no moral outweighing of one of our lives by others so as to lead to a great overall social good. There is no justified sacrifice of some of us for others'.

While Nozick, like **John Locke**, started from the idea of natural rights, he came to different conclusions. For example, he did not consider rights inalienable: people could voluntarily consent to contracts that enslave them, for instance. And he thought Locke was wrong to presume that some sort of social contract was necessary for civil institutions to emerge: as **Adam Ferguson** and **Adam Smith** pointed out, human social psychology is such that mutually beneficial arrangements can and do emerge spontaneously.

Anarcho-capitalists such as **Murray Rothbard** thought that what would emerge, in the absence of force, would be a variety of private agencies, each contracting with people to provide defence and justice services that protect their rights. Nozick, however, argued that there would be no such diversity, because what would ultimately emerge from this spontaneous process would be a single agency providing these services – effectively, a *state*. However, if individuals' basic rights are to remain respected, the power of this state must be limited. It exists only to uphold individuals' rights, protect them from coercion, theft and fraud, and ensure that voluntary contracts are enforced – nothing more. Nozick insisted, however, that this minimal state still maximises the mutual benefit that can be achieved without violating anyone's rights. Nobody could do better by leaving such an arrangement and creating some other of their own.

Anarchy, State and Utopia was a counterblast to John Rawls's *A Theory of Justice*, which used a social contract approach to promote the 'greatest benefit of the least advantaged'. This policy, said Rawls, was necessary to maintain social cohesion. Nozick rejected this as merely Rawls's moral prejudice: as long as nobody's rights were violated, he maintained, the better off have every right to their advantages, as his 'Wilt Chamberlain' example showed. Suppose we start with some 'just' distribution, he suggested; but there is a basketball star called Wilt Chamberlain, and thousands of people willingly pay to see him play. He ends the night with a lot more money, and they end it with a little less. The two are now financially unequal – but the change was purely voluntary. If we start from a just distribution, concluded Nozick, and (as in this case) nobody acts unjustly, then the resulting distribution, however unequal, must also be just. To create and maintain any particular distribution (such as financial equality), the state would not only have to infringe people's rights by forcibly taking from some in order to benefit others; it would have to repeat this injustice every day.

Wealth was not something that simply *exists* to be shared out in this way, insisted Nozick: wealth is something that people *create* through their effort, skill, entrepreneurship and talent. Medical researchers who discover an important cure, for example, have every right to charge what they like for it, because they have harmed no one in the process – only added to beneficial possibilities.

Another of Nozick's examples shows how minimal he believed the state should be. One person works hard and earns money, while the other is penniless from lazing constantly in the sun. Why should we think it any more justifiable to take money (through taxes) from the first than to take leisure time (through forced labour) from the second? There was no difference, Nozick concluded: taxation was a form of slavery and that was a violation of our rights.

[99] Hernando de Soto Polar (1941–): Peruvian economist. **Key idea:** Importance of property rights and institutions in development. **Key works:** *The Other Path: The Invisible Revolution in the Third World* (1986); *The Mystery of Capital* (2000).

The son of a Peruvian diplomat, de Soto and his family took exile in Europe following the 1948 military coup. He returned to Peru thirty years later and established the Institute for Liberty and Democracy, a think tank that would have a significant influence on Peru's economy. Policies included cuts in red tape and the establishment of property rights that allowed some of the poorest Peruvians to start and own businesses legally, rather than being trapped in the informal or 'black' economy.

Over-regulation and the lack of property rights, he argued, made it difficult for people to create legitimate businesses, so they created informal ones instead. But these could not be expanded. Expansion would attract the attention of the (often corrupt) authorities; and with no legal title to their business or even their land or home, poor people had nothing to borrow against in order to invest in their enterprise. Their capital, said de Soto, was *dead capital* – real, but unusable because it was outside the law. Working with governments, de Soto was able to engineer substantial reductions in the paperwork needed to start a business, and to spread property titles to small-scale farmers and entrepreneurs. (The resulting rise in prosperity among some of the poorest Peruvians had the knock-on effect of depriving the country's Shining Path guerrilla movement of support – leading to a bomb attack on de Soto's offices.)

De Soto also argued that people in developed countries take institutions such as property rights, the legal system, impartial justice and access to information for granted. As a result, they cannot understand the plight of people who do not have these things. The legal system, for example, is essential for creating and keeping documents on owner-ship, while open information is essential for trade, enabling people to check prices, credit worthiness, ownership titles and more. In many poorer countries, these benefits are confined to the rich, but a modern market economy depends on them being generally enjoyed.

[100] Deirdre McCloskey (1942–): American economist and historian. **Key idea:** The role of liberal values in economic growth. **Key works:** *The Bourgeois Virtues* (2006); *Bourgeois Dignity* (2010); *Bourgeois Equality* (2016).

The cricket-playing former Marxist Deirdre McCloskey was born male (as Donald McCloskey) but transitioned to female at the age of 53. Her earlier publications included work on price theory and on the use of rhetoric in economics. Her major impact, however, came later, as a result of her study of the economic history of Britain, in which she concluded that the massive economic growth experienced over the last two centuries can be explained not so much by capital or institutions but by the spread of liberal ideas – specifically, 'bourgeois values'.

McCloskey underlined the sheer scale of recent economic growth. In 1800 the average human being earned about $3 a day. Today it is $33 (and that average is weighted down by the large populations of the poorest countries). The population, meanwhile, has grown sevenfold since 1800 – meaning that humanity is producing over seventy times the wealth it did then. Nor is this just a material enrichment: with increasing wealth, longevity and literacy, it is an intellectual and cultural enrichment too.

This *great enrichment* began around 1860. It is not explained by the steady economic growth of Britain since the fourteenth-century Black Death, nor by the Industrial Revolution that began in the late eighteenth century, nor by Britain's institutions and rule of law. Only ideas, she insisted, can change things so much so fast. The great enrichment stemmed from the spread of 'bourgeois liberalism' that allowed ordinary people, for the first time, to enjoy liberty, dignity and prosperity. For centuries until then, commerce had been thought venal and demeaning. But writers such as **John Locke** and **Adam Smith** defended the virtues of freedom, trade, the accumulation of wealth and capital, and the dignity and self-esteem it gave to ordinary citizens. Suddenly, there was nothing to hold back creativity and enterprise.

[101] David D. Friedman (1945–): American anarcho-capitalist economist and legal theorist. **Key ideas:** Anarcho-capitalism; private law; no need for state to agree laws; practical benefits of libertarianism. **Key work:** *The Machinery of Freedom* (1973).

David Friedman is the son of the neoliberal Nobel economist **Milton Friedman** and his wife Rose. His own son, Patri Friedman (1976–), is another libertarian theorist, known for his work on *seasteading*.

Friedman made contributions on price theory and other economic topics, but is known particularly for his *market anarchist* legal theory. He maintained that the state was an unnecessary evil, and that all state services could be better provided by the competitive private economy, including the law itself: 'Producing laws is not an easier job than producing cars and food, so if the government is incompetent to produce cars or food, why do you expect it to do a good job producing the legal system within which you are then going to produce the cars and the food?' In support, he argued that most law is already *private*, with most offences being against (and prosecuted by) private individuals, not the state (as in contract law and the common law). His book *The Machinery of Freedom* (1973) explored this theme.

This approach differed from the other leading anarcho-capitalist **Murray Rothbard**, who imagined that the legal code would have to be agreed by the consent of the parties setting up an anarcho-capitalist community. He also differed from Rothbard in his *consequentialist* argument for market capitalism. While Rothbard justified anarcho-capitalism on the basis of the inviolable natural rights of individuals, Friedman thought that when you analysed the costs and benefits of government action, it was clear that we would be better off without it. And while Rothbard saw libertarianism as a 'revolutionary' movement, Friedman instead favoured the incremental privatisation of government activities, ending with the privatisation of law itself.

11 CONCLUSION

The liberal debate

Liberalism is not an ideology but an ongoing debate. Its focus is to discover how best to maximise individual freedom. Liberals know that human beings are not perfect, nor perfectible; their world cannot be explained by pure principles, nor managed by simple equations. Events are the unpredictable result of the actions – but not always the intentions – of human beings who are often less than rational and far from beneficent. Our best policy is to accept human reality and steer it into beneficial directions.

Liberalism also accepts that human beings are diverse, and seeks to maximise the space and opportunity that they have to pursue their different objectives. It asks how the citizens of so diverse a world can cooperate peacefully together. Its starting position is the freedom of everyone to think, speak, work and pursue their own aims, provided that they do not harm others in the process; and liberals stress the importance of an independent justice system to maintain that order. They support people's freedom to pursue their own ends in their own way, even if self-destructive, without having to ask some authority for permission before doing something. They want to see a personal sphere where the political authorities have no right to interfere with citizens at all. They argue that anyone who wants to curb these freedoms must put up a *very* strong case.

Today's liberals are optimists. They are confident about the free economic order. They maintain that its expansion across the world would bring better education, higher life expectancy, greater longevity, freedom from disease, and more opportunity – particularly to the poorest. Technology and global markets will allow more and more people to sell the fruits of their labour to distant others, boosting specialisation and efficiency. People's desire to improve their own condition through trade with others remains strong.

Is this a liberal world?

Yet, in an age of complexity, uncertainty, volatility and diversity, many people still look to governments for protection and economic security. In response, those governments grow – as does the power and patronage of their politicians and officials. Every liberal knows the dangers of that.

Liberals have still not succeeded in making those in power understand and accept the limits of their legitimate authority. Yet support for economic, political and social freedom is spreading throughout the world, thanks in large part to improved travel, education and communications – and the case for these freedoms that has been made by generations of gifted liberal thinkers who understand the creative genius of a free people.

12 101 MORE LIBERAL QUOTATIONS

[1] To lead the people, walk behind them.   Laozi

[2] Just because you do not take an interest in politics doesn't mean politics won't take an interest in you.   Pericles

[3] Freedom is the sure possession of those alone who have the courage to defend it.   Pericles

[4] Beware the man of a single book.   Thomas Aquinas

[5] A free man is he that, in those things which by his strength and wit he is able to do, is not hindered to do what he has a will to.   Thomas Hobbes

[6] The right of nature ... is the liberty each man hath to use his own power, as he will himself, for the preservation of his own nature; that is to say, of his own life.

Thomas Hobbes

[7] No man who knows aught, can be so stupid to deny that all men naturally were born free.   John Milton

[8] The only ends for which governments are constituted, and obedience rendered to them, are the obtaining of justice and protection; and they who cannot provide for both give the people a right of taking such ways as best please themselves, in order to their own safety.   Algernon Sidney

[9] Men being by nature all free, equal and independent, no one can be put out of his estate and subjected to the

political power of another without his own consent, which is done by agreeing with other men, to join and unite into a community for their comfortable, safe, and peaceable living in a secure enjoyment of their properties.

John Locke

[10] [H]e that thinks absolute power purifies men's blood, and corrects the baseness of human nature, need read the history of this, or any other age, to be convinced to the contrary.   John Locke

[11] [E]very man has a property in his own person. This nobody has any right to but himself. The labour of his body, and the work of his hands, we may say, are properly his ... The great and chief end, therefore, of mens' uniting into commonwealths, and putting themselves under government, is the preservation of their property.   John Locke

[12] Alas! Power encroaches daily upon liberty, with a success too evident; and the balance between them is almost lost. Tyranny has engrossed almost the whole earth, and striking at mankind root and branch, makes the world a slaughter-house; and will certainly go on to destroy, till it is either destroyed itself, or, which is most likely, has left nothing else to destroy.   Thomas Gordon

[13] I flatter my self to have demonstrated that, neither the friendly qualities and kind affections that are natural to man, nor the real virtues he is capable of acquiring by reason and self-denial, are the foundation of society; but that what we call evil in this world, moral as well as natural, is the grand principle that makes us sociable creatures, the solid basis, the life and support of all trades and employments without exception: that there we must look for the true origin of all arts and sciences, and that the moment evil ceases, the society must be spoiled, if not totally dissolved.   Bernard Mandeville

[14]   In the state of nature ... all men are born equal, but they cannot continue in this equality. Society makes them lose it, and they recover it only by the protection of the law.

Montesquieu

[15]   [C]onstant experience shows us that every man who has power is inclined to abuse it; he goes until he finds limits.

Montesquieu

[16]   The art of government is to make two-thirds of a nation pay all it possibly can pay for the benefit of the other third.

Voltaire

[17]   Without freedom of thought there can be no such thing as wisdom; and no such thing as public liberty without freedom of speech.   Benjamin Franklin

[18]   Freedom of speech is a principal pillar of a free government; when this support is taken away, the constitution of a free society is dissolved, and tyranny is erected on its ruins.   Benjamin Franklin

[19]   It is seldom that liberty of any kind is lost all at once ... But if the liberty of the press ever be lost, it must be lost at once.

David Hume

[20]   It is the highest impertinence and presumption, therefore, in kings and ministers to pretend to watch over the economy of private people, and to restrain their expense. ... They are themselves always, and without exception, the greatest spendthrifts in the society. Let them look well after their own expense, and they may safely trust private people with theirs.   Adam Smith

[21]   Little else is requisite to carry a state to the highest degree of opulence from the lowest barbarism, but peace, easy taxes and a tolerable administration of justice; all the rest being brought about by the natural course of things.

Adam Smith

[22] By pursuing his own interest [every individual] frequently promotes that of the society more effectually than when he really intends to promote it.   Adam Smith

[23] The natural effort of every individual to better his own condition ... is so powerful, that it is alone, and without any assistance, not only capable of carrying on the society to wealth and prosperity, but of surmounting a hundred impertinent obstructions with which the folly of human laws too often encumbers its operations.   Adam Smith

[24] The function of the just state is to impose the minimum restrictions and safeguard the maximum liberties of the people, and it never regards the person as a thing.

Immanuel Kant

[25] The enjoyment of power inevitably corrupts the judgment of reason, and perverts its liberty.   Immanuel Kant

[26] The exercise of one coercion always makes another inevitable.   Anders Chydenius

[27] He that would make his own liberty secure must guard even his enemy from oppression; for if he violates this duty he establishes a precedent that will reach to himself.

Thomas Paine

[28] For a punishment to be just it should consist of only such gradations of intensity as suffice to deter men from committing crimes.   Cesare Beccaria

[29] I have sworn upon the altar of God, eternal hostility against every form of tyranny over the mind of man.

Thomas Jefferson

[30] The spirit of resistance to government is so valuable on certain occasions, that I wish it to be always kept alive. It will often be exercised when wrong, but better so than not to be exercised at all.   Thomas Jefferson

[31] As to the evil which results from a censorship, it is impossible to measure it, for it is impossible to tell where it ends.
Jeremy Bentham

[32] Among the several cloudy appellatives which have been commonly employed as cloaks for misgovernment, there is none more conspicuous in this atmosphere of illusion than the word 'order'.
Jeremy Bentham

[33] The accumulation of all powers, legislative, executive, and judiciary, in the same hands, whether of one, a few, or many, and whether hereditary, self-appointed, or elective, may justly be pronounced the very definition of tyranny.
James Madison

[34] [A]ll power is originally vested in, and consequently derived from, the people. That government is instituted and ought to be exercised for the benefit of the people; which consists in the enjoyment of life and liberty and the right of acquiring property, and generally of pursuing and obtaining happiness and safety.
James Madison

[35] Crisis is the rallying cry of the tyrant.   James Madison

[36] Great power often corrupts virtue; it invariably renders vice more malignant ... In proportion as the powers of government increase, both its own character and that of the people becomes worse.
John Taylor of Caroline

[37] Government will not fail to employ education to strengthen its hands and perpetuate its institutions.
William Godwin

[38] Government regulations are all coercive to some degree, and even when they are not, they habituate man to expect teaching, guidance and help outside himself, instead of formulating his own.
Wilhelm von Humboldt

[39] Every time government attempts to handle our affairs, it costs more and the results are worse than if we had handled them ourselves. Benjamin Constant

[40] There is a bizarre notion according to which it is claimed that because men are corrupt, it is necessary to give certain of them all the more power ... on the contrary, they must be given less power. Benjamin Constant

[41] The property a man has in his own industry is violated, whenever he is forbidden the free exercise of his faculties or talents, except insomuch as they would interfere with the rights of third parties. Jean Baptiste Say

[42] Experience, however, shows that neither a state nor a bank ever have [sic] had the unrestricted power of issuing paper money without abusing that power; in all states, therefore, the issue of paper money ought to be under some check and control; and none seems so proper for that purpose as that of subjecting the issuers of paper money to the obligation of paying their notes either in gold coin or bullion. David Ricardo

[43] I call that mind free, which jealously guards its intellectual rights and powers, which calls no man master, which does not content itself with a passive or hereditary faith, which opens itself to light whencesoever it may come. William Ellery Channing

[44] The doctrine of blind obedience and unqualified submission to any human power, whether civil or ecclesiastical, is the doctrine of despotism, and ought to have no place among Republicans and Christians. Angelina Grimké

[45] As long as the law may be diverted from its true purpose – that it may violate property instead of protecting it – then everyone will want to participate in making the law, either to protect himself against plunder or to use it for plunder.

Political questions will always be prejudicial, dominant, and all-absorbing. There will be fighting to gain access to the legislature as well as fighting within it.

Frédéric Bastiat

[46] Life, liberty and property do not exist because men have made laws. On the contrary, it was the fact that life, liberty and property existed beforehand that caused men to make laws in the first place. Frédéric Bastiat

[47] Now, legal plunder can be committed in an infinite number of ways. Thus we have an infinite number of plans for organising it: tariffs, protection, benefits, subsidies, encouragements, progressive taxation, public schools, guaranteed jobs, guaranteed profits, minimum wages, a right to relief, a right to the tools of labour, free credit, and so on... Frédéric Bastiat

[48] Force is not a remedy. John Bright

[49] Democracy extends the sphere of individual freedom, socialism restricts it. Democracy attaches all possible value to each man; socialism makes each man a mere agent, a mere number. Democracy and socialism have nothing in common but one word: equality. But notice the difference: while democracy seeks equality in liberty, socialism seeks equality in restraint and servitude.

Alexis de Tocqueville

[50] The American Republic will endure, until politicians realise they can bribe the people with their own money.

Alexis de Tocqueville

[51] Enslave the liberty of but one human being and the liberties of the world are put in peril.

William Lloyd Garrison

[52] If all mankind minus one were of one opinion, mankind would be no more justified in silencing that one person

than he, if he had the power, would be justified in silencing mankind. John Stuart Mill

[53] The only freedom deserving the name, is that of pursuing our own good in our own way, so long as we do not attempt to deprive others of theirs, or impede their efforts to obtain it. John Stuart Mill

[54] The principle that the majority have a right to rule the minority, practically resolves all government into a mere contest between two bodies of men, as to which of them shall be masters, and which of them slaves...

Lysander Spooner

[55] Vices are not crimes. Lysander Spooner

[56] [N]o government, so called, can reasonably be trusted, or reasonably be supposed to have honest purposes in view, any longer than it depends wholly upon voluntary support.

Lysander Spooner

[57] I am truly free only when all human beings, men and women, are equally free. The freedom of other men, far from negating or limiting my freedom, is, on the contrary, its necessary premise and confirmation.

Mikhael Bakunin

[58] Do you want to make it impossible for anyone to oppress his fellow-man? Then make sure that no one shall possess power. Mikhael Bakunin

[59] The liberty of man consists solely in this, that he obeys the laws of nature because he has himself recognised them as such, and not because they have been imposed upon him externally by any foreign will whatsoever, human or divine, collective or individual. Mikhael Bakunin

[60] If a thousand men were not to pay their tax-bills this year, that would not be a violent and bloody measure, as it would

be to pay them, and enable the State to commit violence and shed innocent blood. This is, in fact, the definition of a peaceable revolution, if any such is possible.

Henry David Thoreau

[61] There will never be a really free and enlightened State until the State comes to recognize the individual as a higher and independent power, from which all its own power and authority are derived, and treats him accordingly.

Henry David Thoreau

[62] To suppress free speech is a double wrong. It violates the rights of the hearer as well as those of the speaker.

Frederick Douglass

[63] I know no class of my fellowmen, however just, enlightened, and humane, which can be wisely and safely trusted absolutely with the liberties of any other class.

Frederick Douglass

[64] Just as war is the natural consequence of monopoly, peace is the natural consequence of liberty.

Gustave de Molinari

[65] A man's liberties are none the less aggressed upon because those who coerce him do so in the belief that he will be benefited.
Herbert Spencer

[66] By liberty I mean the assurance that every man shall be protected in doing what he believes is his duty against the influence of authority and majorities, custom and opinion.

Lord Acton

[67] The most certain test by which we judge whether a country is really free is the amount of security enjoyed by minorities.
Lord Acton

[68] [E]very tax or rate, forcibly taken from an unwilling person, is immoral and oppressive.
Auberon Herbert

[69] Government should be repressive no further than is necessary to secure liberty by protecting the equal rights of each from aggression on the part of others, and the moment governmental prohibitions extend beyond this line they are in danger of defeating the very ends they are intended to serve.   Henry George

[70] It has ever been the tendency of power to add to itself, to enlarge its sphere, to encroach beyond the limits set for it; and where the habit of resisting such encroachment is not fostered, and the individual is not taught to be jealous of his rights, individuality gradually disappears and the government or State becomes the all-in-all.

Benjamin Tucker

[71] [J]ust as the monopolist of a food product often furnishes poison instead of nutriment, so the State takes advantage of its monopoly of defense to furnish invasion instead of protection; that, just as the patrons of the one pay to be poisoned, so the patrons of the other pay to be enslaved; and, finally, that the State exceeds all its fellow-monopolists in the extent of its villainy because it enjoys the unique privilege of compelling all people to buy its product whether they want it or not.   Benjamin Tucker

[72] Make no laws whatever concerning speech, and speech will be free; so soon as you make a declaration on paper that speech shall be free, you will have a hundred lawyers proving that 'freedom does not mean abuse, nor liberty license', and they will define freedom out of existence.

Voltairine de Cleyre

[73] The State ... both in its genesis and by its primary intention, is purely anti-social. It is not based on the idea of natural rights, but on the idea that the individual has no rights except those that the State may provisionally grant him.

Albert Jay Nock

[74] Once the principle is admitted that it is the duty of the government to protect the individual against his own foolishness, no serious objections can be advanced against further encroachments. Ludwig von Mises

[75] The champions of socialism call themselves progressives, but they recommend a system which is characterized by rigid observance of routine and by a resistance to every kind of improvement. They call themselves liberals, but they are intent upon abolishing liberty. They call themselves democrats, but they yearn for dictatorship. They call themselves revolutionaries, but they want to make the government omnipotent. They promise the blessings of the Garden of Eden, but they plan to transform the world into a gigantic post office. Every man but one a subordinate clerk in a bureau. Ludwig von Mises

[76] A tax supported, compulsory educational system is the complete model of the totalitarian state.

Isabel Paterson

[77] No state, no government exists. What does in fact exist is a man, or a few men, in power over many men.

Rose Wilder Lane

[78] No human being, man, woman, or child, may safely be entrusted to the power of another; for no human being may safely be trusted with absolute power.

Suzanne La Follette

[79] If experience teaches anything, it is that what the community undertakes to do is usually done badly. This is due in part to the temptation to corruption that such enterprises involve, but even more, perhaps, to the lack of personal interest on the part of those engaged in them.

Suzanne La Follette

[80] The curious task of economics is to demonstrate to men how little they really know about what they imagine they can design.   F. A. Hayek

[81] The argument for liberty is not an argument against organization, which is one of the most powerful tools human reason can employ, but an argument against all exclusive, privileged, monopolistic organization, against the use of coercion to prevent others from doing better.

F. A. Hayek

[82] The smallest minority on earth is the individual. Those who deny individual rights, cannot claim to be defenders of minorities. Individual rights are not subject to a public vote; a majority has no right to vote away the rights of a minority; the political function of rights is precisely to protect minorities from oppression by majorities.

Ayn Rand

[83] I swear by my life, and love of it, that I will never live for the sake of another man, nor ask another man to live for mine.

Ayn Rand

[84] Those who have ever valued liberty for its own sake believed that to be free to choose, and not to be chosen for, is an unalienable ingredient in what makes human beings human.   Isaiah Berlin

[85] An important reason may be that government at the present time is so large that it has reached the stage of negative marginal productivity, which means that any additional function it takes on will probably result in more harm than good...   Ronald Coase

[86] A society that puts equality ... ahead of freedom will end up with neither equality nor freedom.   Milton Friedman

[87] The preservation of freedom is the protective reason for limiting and decentralizing governmental power. But

there is also a constructive reason. The great advances of civilization, whether in architecture or painting, in science or in literature, in industry or agriculture, have never come from centralized government.   Milton Friedman

[88] Concentrated power is not rendered harmless by the good intentions of those who create it.   Milton Friedman

[89] I'm in favor of legalizing drugs. According to my value system, if people want to kill themselves, they have every right to do so. Most of the harm that comes from drugs is because they are illegal.   Milton Friedman

[90] Nothing is so permanent as a temporary government program.   Milton Friedman

[91] Politicians and bureaucrats are no different from the rest of us. They will maximize their incentives just like everybody else.   James M. Buchanan

[92] The great non sequitur committed by defenders of the State ... is to leap from the necessity of society to the necessity of the State.   Murray Rothbard

[93] The world's problem is not too many people, but lack of political and economic freedom.   Julian Simon

[94] As long as a single center has a monopoly on the use of coercion, one has a state rather than a self-governed society.   Elinor Ostrom

[95] But let me offer you my definition of social justice: I keep what I earn and you keep what you earn. Do you disagree? Well then tell me how much of what I earn belongs to you – and why?   Walter Williams

[96] Democracy and liberty are not the same. Democracy is little more than mob rule, while liberty refers to the sovereignty of the individual.   Walter Williams

[97] Prior to capitalism, the way people amassed great wealth was by looting, plundering and enslaving their fellow man. Capitalism made it possible to become wealthy by serving your fellow man.   Walter Williams

[98] Taxation of earnings from labor is on a par with forced labor. Seizing the results of someone's labor is equivalent to seizing hours from him and directing him to carry on various activities.   Robert Nozick

[99] Nor during the Age of Innovation have the poor gotten poorer, as people are always saying. On the contrary, the poor have been the chief beneficiaries of modern capitalism. It is an irrefutable historical finding, obscured by the logical truth that the profits from innovation go in the first act mostly to the bourgeois rich.   Deirdre McCloskey

[100] That businesspeople buy low and sell high in a particularly alert and advantageous way does not make them bad unless all trading is bad, unless when you yourself shop prudently you are bad, unless any tall poppy needs to be cut down, unless we wish to run our ethical lives on the sin of envy.   Deirdre McCloskey

[101] Property is a central economic institution of any society, and private property is the central institution of a free society.   David D. Friedman

ABOUT THE IEA

The Institute is a research and educational charity (No. CC 235 351), limited by guarantee. Its mission is to improve understanding of the fundamental institutions of a free society by analysing and expounding the role of markets in solving economic and social problems.

The IEA achieves its mission by:

- a high-quality publishing programme
- conferences, seminars, lectures and other events
- outreach to school and college students
- brokering media introductions and appearances

The IEA, which was established in 1955 by the late Sir Antony Fisher, is an educational charity, not a political organisation. It is independent of any political party or group and does not carry on activities intended to affect support for any political party or candidate in any election or referendum, or at any other time. It is financed by sales of publications, conference fees and voluntary donations.

In addition to its main series of publications, the IEA also publishes (jointly with the University of Buckingham), *Economic Affairs*.

The IEA is aided in its work by a distinguished international Academic Advisory Council and an eminent panel of Honorary Fellows. Together with other academics, they review prospective IEA publications, their comments being passed on anonymously to authors. All IEA papers are therefore subject to the same rigorous independent refereeing process as used by leading academic journals.

IEA publications enjoy widespread classroom use and course adoptions in schools and universities. They are also sold throughout the world and often translated/reprinted.

Since 1974 the IEA has helped to create a worldwide network of 100 similar institutions in over 70 countries. They are all independent but share the IEA's mission.

Views expressed in the IEA's publications are those of the authors, not those of the Institute (which has no corporate view), its Managing Trustees, Academic Advisory Council members or senior staff.

Members of the Institute's Academic Advisory Council, Honorary Fellows, Trustees and Staff are listed on the following page.

The Institute gratefully acknowledges financial support for its publications programme and other work from a generous benefaction by the late Professor Ronald Coase.

The Institute of Economic Affairs
2 Lord North Street, Westminster, London SW1P 3LB
Tel: 020 7799 8900
Fax: 020 7799 2137
Email: iea@iea.org.uk
Internet: iea.org.uk

Institute of
Economic Affairs

Other IEA publications

Comprehensive information on other publications and the wider work of the IEA can be found at www.iea.org.uk. To order any publication please see below.

Personal customers

Orders from personal customers should be directed to the IEA:

Clare Rusbridge
IEA
2 Lord North Street
FREEPOST LON10168
London SW1P 3YZ
Tel: 020 7799 8907. Fax: 020 7799 2137
Email: sales@iea.org.uk

Trade customers

All orders from the book trade should be directed to the IEA's distributor:

NBN International (IEA Orders)
Orders Dept.
NBN International
10 Thornbury Road
Plymouth PL6 7PP
Tel: 01752 202301, Fax: 01752 202333
Email: orders@nbninternational.com

IEA subscriptions

The IEA also offers a subscription service to its publications. For a single annual payment (currently £42.00 in the UK), subscribers receive every monograph the IEA publishes. For more information please contact:

Clare Rusbridge
Subscriptions
IEA
2 Lord North Street
FREEPOST LON10168
London SW1P 3YZ
Tel: 020 7799 8907, Fax: 020 7799 2137
Email: crusbridge@iea.org.uk